T0322142

JOHN SELLARS

Aristotle
Understanding the World's Greatest Philosopher

A PELICAN BOOK

PELICAN
an imprint of
PENGUIN BOOKS

PELICAN BOOKS

UK | USA | Canada | Ireland | Australia
India | New Zealand | South Africa

Penguin Books is part of the Penguin Random
House group of companies whose addresses can
be found at global.penguinrandomhouse.com

Penguin
Random House
UK

First published 2023
Published in paperback 2024
003

Book design by Matthew Young
Set in 11/16.13pt FreightText Pro
Typeset by Jouve (UK), Milton Keynes
Printed and bound in Great Britain by
Clays Ltd, Elcograf S.p.A.

The authorized representative in the EEA is
Penguin Random House Ireland, Morrison
Chambers, 32 Nassau Street, Dublin D02 YH68

A CIP catalogue record for this book is available
from the British Library

ISBN: 978-0-241-61564-5

MIX
Paper | Supporting
responsible forestry
FSC® C018179

For Richard

Contents

Introduction

In 1996, work began on a new Museum of Modern Art in Athens. An ideal site had been secured not far from the Hellenic Parliament, next door to the Byzantine and Christian Museum and just over the street from the Museum of Cycladic Art. A building had been designed by the internationally renowned architect I. M. Pei. As work commenced to prepare the site, archaeologists came in to assess anything that might be uncovered. In a city like Athens, the odds of finding interesting artefacts were quite high. Even so, no one was expecting to find what they did. On the face of it, what they unearthed was not especially inspiring: the foundations of a rectangular courtyard surrounded on three sides by covered walkways, with some smaller rooms behind. The size and layout of the buildings were remarkably similar to the remains of gymnasium buildings uncovered at the Academy, one of three gymnasia that existed just outside the walls of the ancient city of Athens. Given the location of this new site, just east of the ancient city, it was quickly identified as the site of the Lyceum, described by a number of ancient writers. Once the identification had been made, all plans for the new museum were halted and the remains were left visible. The archaeological site is now open to the public.

In Athens, as in many historic cities in Europe, almost every building site has layers of important archaeology underneath it. Not all of them can be left exposed. Why was this one deemed to be so important? One of the information boards at the site explains why, commenting that 'it is difficult to appreciate, from the scant archaeological remains on this site, that this spot is one of the most significant places in the history of mankind.' This is because the Lyceum was not merely a gymnasium, not just a place for physical exercise; it was also the home of the philosophical school of Aristotle, one of the greatest thinkers who ever lived. It was here, towards the end of his life, that Aristotle gathered with like-minded friends and pupils to think about and reflect on a dizzying array of topics, from abstract questions in philosophy, the study of the natural world, and the foundations of logic, to rhetoric, drama, politics, and more. Together at the Lyceum they lived the life of the mind, absorbed in intellectual inquiry.

In one of his works, Aristotle describes the immense pleasure that can be gained from this sort of inquiry; he clearly loved what he did. However, he did not do it simply because he happened to enjoy it. He thought that this was the highest activity that any human could do. Indeed, he argued that it is something that we all should do, at least from time to time. In his *Exhortation to Philosophy* (*Protrepticus*) – an early work now surviving only in fragments – he argued not only that we ought to do philosophy but also that it is the *only* route to a fully happy life. A life completely devoid of this kind of intellectual activity is, he believed, barely worth living. This is because it is an expression of our natural human curiosity, and so if we neglect it there is a sense in which we fail to live properly human lives. While few of us will ever reach the intellectual heights of Aristotle, most of us pause from time to time to think about big questions, such as what will make us happy, or what matters most in life. Many of us experience wonder at the beauty and complexity of the natural world, if only via documentaries on television. In these small ways, we participate in the same activity as Aristotle and his companions did at the Lyceum almost two and a half thousand years ago.

Ever since then, Aristotle's ideas and concepts have seeped into our natural ways of thinking, to the point of becoming imperceptible. His work studying animals on the island of Lesbos and elsewhere in the mid-fourth century BC in effect created the discipline of biology and – along with his wider reflections about the nature of knowledge – laid the foundation for all empirical science. He was also the first person to study the structures of rational thought, inventing formal logic in the process, and articulating for the first time key logical principles, such as the law of the excluded middle: any proposition is either true or false. That binary division is the foundational idea that stands behind the digital world that we increasingly inhabit. His examination of different types of political organization and the constitutions of ancient cities inaugurated the discipline of political science. His analysis of Greek drama set out the core elements of successful storytelling – ideas that continue to influence Hollywood scriptwriters today.

Aristotle's influence has been enormous, not only shaping philosophy and science throughout the Middle Ages in the Greek, Syriac, Arabic, Hebrew, and Latin traditions, but continuing indirectly to impact on how we think and live today. Inevitably his reputation has had periods of rise and fall over the years. When a significant number of his works were rediscovered by the philosophers and theologians of Latin Europe in the twelfth and thirteenth centuries via translations from Arabic and Greek, he was seen as a dangerous radical and many of his ideas were quickly condemned by the Church. But when, a few centuries later, his ideas had been accommodated within Christian theology and the study of his works had become the mainstay of university education, he was seen as an overbearing figure of authority who stifled free inquiry and held back the rise of modern science. More perceptive critics could see that the problem was with excessive deference to Aristotle's words by Aristotelians of the day rather than with Aristotle himself. Even so, that image of Aristotle as an immense authority figure has not entirely gone away. It is not helped by the fact that many of his works can be challenging to read. As one of his translators has commented, 'Aristotle is terse, compact, abrupt, his arguments condensed, his thought dense.' It's not surprising that readers approaching him for the first time can feel intimidated.

It would be a great shame, however, if this stopped people from trying to learn more about Aristotle's ideas, which have proved so influential. I suggest that we should all aspire to know at least something about these ideas and how they have shaped the way we think about things today. That is not to say that we all ought to embrace everything that he said and become card-carrying Aristotelians. That would be a decidedly un-Aristotelian outcome. He would not want us to accept his ideas as a fixed body of knowledge. Many of the claims he makes are provisional; they are tentative proposals, open to criticism and subject to rejection should new evidence appear. He sometimes approaches the same problem more than once, giving seemingly conflicting answers. All this underlines the fact that he certainly wasn't a dogmatic thinker and that his works don't necessarily form a comprehensive, monolithic system – even though it is so easy to see them that way. Aristotle wasn't a rigid system builder; he was an inquirer, a man in pursuit of knowledge, restlessly in search of answers to every conceivable question.

Aristotle's great teacher Plato nicknamed him 'the mind', on account of his impressive, ever-hungry intellect. There is, then, a double meaning in the phrase 'the life of the mind': it can refer to the life of Aristotle himself, 'the mind', and it can refer to the sort of life that he led, devoted to the pursuit of knowledge and understanding. In this book, as we follow the trajectory of Aristotle's own life and explore some of the most important ideas in his work, we shall get a sense of both. Aristotle wrote a lot and we won't be able to examine all his works here; those that we will encounter won't be discussed in the depth they deserve. This is simply a taste, an opportunity to get a flavour of who Aristotle was, what he thought, and the vast impact he has had on how we think about ourselves and everything around us. One central idea that we shall return to is that we too should embrace 'the life of the mind', at least from time to time. As we shall see, Aristotle will argue that only by doing this will we be able to enjoy rich and meaningful lives. It is, he argues, a vital part of what it means to be human. Only the person who makes full use of their capacity to understand, he insists, is truly alive.

CHAPTER 1
The Contemplative Life

'All humans by nature desire to know.' So opens Aristotle's book *Metaphysics*, emphatically stating what he believed to be one of our defining characteristics: we are all naturally curious. As small children we all continually ask the question 'why?' and as adults we all cultivate our own private passions that lead us to amass vast amounts of often useless information about whatever grabs our attention, whether that be stamp collecting, family history, football results, birdwatching, or something else. Why do we do this? Aristotle's answer is straightforward: it's simply what human beings do. We can't help being curious. We don't do this for any further purpose or utility; we just do it. To be a human being is to want to know things. But, he would argue, it ought not to be merely a matter of gathering facts; the ultimate goal is not simply to know lots of useless information, but instead to use that information to help us *understand* the world around us.

The *Metaphysics* isn't really a book at all, in the sense of being a single, coherent work. Instead, it's a collection of fourteen shorter texts, which are themselves usually referred to as 'books'. Each of these ancient books probably corresponded to the contents of a single papyrus scroll. Some of them may have been based on lecture notes prepared by

Aristotle himself, but not intended for wider publication. According to ancient tradition, after Aristotle's death his lecture notes were passed on to his pupil Theophrastus, who in turn left them to his pupil Neleus, who left them to a relative who had no great interest in philosophy. They were stored in an underground tunnel, perhaps to keep them hidden from officials who were searching for books to take to the recently founded library at Pergamum. After a century or so, these now-mouldy manuscripts again saw the light of day when one of Neleus' descendants sold them to a book collector called Apellicon of Teos. Apellicon had them copied, restoring damaged parts of the texts and probably introducing all sorts of corruptions in the process. After Apellicon had died, the Roman general Sulla is said to have taken them from Athens to Rome in the first century BC, where they were copied again, put into some kind of order, and prepared for publication. A series of texts dealing with questions about the natural world were grouped together under the title *Physics*, and a further group dealing with more fundamental questions about the nature of things were put 'after the *Physics*', *meta ta Physica*, and so gained the title *Metaphysics*. The word 'metaphysics' doesn't, then, refer to anything supernatural or beyond the physical; it's not a word that Aristotle ever would have used either. He described the topics that he discusses in the *Metaphysics* as 'first philosophy' – the study of the most general and fundamental features of everything that exists. These are in many ways the most important questions we can ask, because they apply to absolutely everything.

Aristotle first began to reflect on these sorts of questions while a student in Plato's Academy. He was born in Stagira, a town in northern Greece, in 384 BC. His father, who may have been a doctor, died when Aristotle was about ten years old. In the wake of this, Aristotle came under the protection of a guardian, Proxenus, who had himself studied at the Academy. And so, around the age of seventeen or eighteen, Aristotle was sent off to Athens to do the same. We don't know if Proxenus inspired the young Aristotle to pursue this path with tales of Athenian intellectual life, or if he was simply sent off regardless of his own wishes.

Aristotle would spend twenty years at the Academy. Situated just north-west of the ancient city of Athens, the Academy was the gymnasium where Plato taught for a number of years. This would have been a relatively quiet, secluded spot, well away from the Agora or marketplace in the centre of Athens where Plato's own teacher, Socrates, had held his philosophical discussions. Socrates was accused, tried, and ultimately executed by the Athenian authorities for his troublesome questioning; it is perhaps no wonder that Plato opted for a more discreet location. The Academy was originally a religious site and had become a place for athletic training, so it was already in a sense a centre of education. In time, Plato acquired a property near the Academy gymnasium and this became the base of operations for what we now refer to as 'Plato's Academy'. Aristotle probably arrived around the time that this happened.

During this period, Plato was deeply immersed in metaphysical questions, writing among other things his dialogue *Parmenides*. This work was named after a philosopher who may justly be called the founding father of metaphysics. Parmenides was from the city of Elea in southern Italy. Plato had spent time in the Greek cities of southern Italy and Sicily where he encountered the ideas of Parmenides and Pythagoras among others. Indeed, he had just returned to Athens from a trip to Sicily when he bought his property at the Academy and welcomed the teenage Aristotle as a new student. The dialogue *Parmenides* is set well in the past, and in it Plato portrays an elderly Parmenides visiting Athens for a festival and meeting the young Socrates. Whether such an encounter ever really took place (or was even chronologically possible), we do not know. In the ensuing discussion, Plato's character Parmenides recounts his own distinctive views about the nature of what exists, views which the real Parmenides had outlined and defended in a poem.

What did Parmenides say in this poem? It is a challenging text which is difficult to interpret but, in effect, it is a reflection on what it means for something *to be*, or what it means to say that something *is*. He writes, deeply enigmatically, that 'what is cannot not be'. This is of course simply a tautology: if something *is*, then it cannot also be *is not*. But Parmenides doesn't tell us what it is that *is*. He then quickly adds that 'what is not must not be'. In other words, what *is not* is impossible. How could you ever encounter something that *is not*? Even if it were possible, how could you describe it? After all, this would be something that doesn't exist, that isn't there. There's a sharp division, then, between what *is* and what *is not*. What *is* must necessarily exist, because it 'cannot not be', while what *is not* is impossible. Even if you think of something seemingly unreal – say a unicorn – you'll be thinking of *something*, which exists at least as the object of your thought. If it didn't exist, how could you even think about it? So, what *is* – whatever that might be – necessarily *is* and what *is not* is impossible, literally inconceivable. If what *is not* is impossible, then everything must fall into the category of what *is* and so everything necessarily exists.

This is how metaphysics begins, with this incredibly abstract reflection on what it means to say that something *is*. Parmenides' poem is the oldest extended piece of philosophical writing that survives; it is the oldest text we have that does not merely assert things but offers reasons for its claims. It goes on to make the following arguments. First, what *is* (or exists) is ungenerated and indestructible. It has to be, because otherwise it would have to come into being out of what *is not*. Yet, as we have already seen, what *is not* is impossible. Moreover, how could something suddenly come into being out of what *is not*? What could have prompted this creation *ex nihilo*? There would have had to have been at least some cause to prompt this miraculous event. So, what *is* (or exists) not only necessarily exists but has always existed, was never created, and will never be destroyed. (If it were destroyed, we'd be faced with what *is not*, which Parmenides has already told us is impossible.) Second, what *is* (or exists) is a single, unified thing. There cannot be more than one thing that exists, because in order to distinguish one from another there would have to be some 'what is not' (non-existence) in between them. Yet what is not is impossible, so that can't be the case. Third, if what *is* (or exists) is a single, unified entity – equally *is* throughout – then there can be no change within it. No one part can change (into non-existence) and, as we have already seen, the whole thing has existed eternally. On the basis of this analysis, Parmenides seems to have concluded that for anything to exist at all it must be both eternal and unchanging. The further, more disturbing conclusion seems to be that the world of variety, plurality, and change that we are all familiar with must in fact be an illusion, because what really exists is this single, unchanging, eternal entity – an entity that we can only comprehend by reflecting on the meaning of what it means to say that something *is*. The way we uncover the truth about what exists is not via our senses, then, but by the use of reason.

These reflections about the nature of being profoundly influenced Plato and shaped discussions in the Academy. Around the same time that Parmenides was writing his poem in Elea, another philosopher on the other side of the ancient Mediterranean made some quite different claims which would prove to be equally important. His name was Heraclitus and he was from the city of Ephesus in Asia Minor. In contrast to Parmenides, who had argued that ultimately nothing ever really changes, Heraclitus claimed that *everything* is in a continual process of transformation, never the same from one moment to the next. Famously, he is reported to have said that 'it is impossible to step into the same river twice'. Plato himself quoted this saying in another of his dialogues, the *Cratylus*, named after one of his teachers. Cratylus had once been a pupil of Heraclitus and developed a fairly extreme interpretation of his master's philosophy. He argued, according to Plato, that if everything is continually changing, as Heraclitus had said, then nothing is ever the same from one moment to the next. If that's the case, then can we ever really say anything about anything? Can we ever pin anything down long enough to determine what it is? Even if we do, will it have transformed into something else by the time we try to say anything about it? If Heraclitus was right, and everything is indeed continually changing, then can we ever know anything at all? More disturbingly, can we ever *say* anything? According to Aristotle in the *Metaphysics*, Cratylus thought not and gave up on speech altogether, reduced to wagging his finger. Whereas Heraclitus had said that it is impossible to step into the same river twice, because the water is always changing, Cratylus said that it is impossible to step into same river even once, because ultimately there is no river.

These two very different influences shaped Plato's own metaphysics. Yet, despite their differences, they pointed in the same direction. Cratylus' version of Heraclitus' philosophy denied that it was ever possible to have secure knowledge of the ever-changing natural world, because we can never pin it down for long enough to grasp it. Parmenides then offered a way out of that conundrum by arguing that it is through reason, not the senses, that we can come to know what truly exists, which is unchanging and eternal. It was in the light of these ideas that Plato developed his celebrated theory of ideal forms. In a number of his dialogues, Plato suggested that the objects that we encounter in the changing physical world are but copies of more perfect, unchanging ideal forms. These unchanging forms are eternal, embodying many of the characteristics that Parmenides associated with existence, and as such they avoid Cratylus' concerns about the possibility of knowledge. Because they never change, they can be secure objects of knowledge. Whenever we encounter a particular entity, say, a horse, we recognize it as a horse because it in some way participates in the idea or concept of horse or horseness. Not only that, in order for us to recognize a particular horse as a horse we must already have that idea within us, which is to say that we must have already encountered the idea of horseness at some point before we started experiencing the world. This led Plato to suggest that our souls, before being conjoined with our bodies, must have had some kind of disembodied encounter with the ideal forms of things.

As far-fetched as it sounds, Plato did indeed outline this scenario, but he did so tentatively, putting it into the mouths of characters in his dialogues rather than saying it in his own voice. For the most part, it is Socrates who stands as Plato's mouthpiece, presenting this theory of ideal forms. Elsewhere Plato wrote things that seem flatly to contradict those claims, and nowhere more so than in his late dialogue *Parmenides*. In this dialogue, it is the great Parmenides who takes centre stage to explain to a young Socrates all the problems that such a theory faces. It's all very complex dramatically: are we supposed now to think that Socrates all along knew the problems facing the theory, given that he was told them in his youth? Or are we supposed to think that the mature Socrates found a way to overcome these objections? Among the problems that Parmenides raises – although of course this is Plato writing – is the following: in what sense can particular objects like horses participate in the idea of horseness? Is there a little bit of the ideal form of horse in each and every living horse? If so, that suggests that the idea has been divided and resides in multiple spatial locations at once. But how can an immaterial idea do that? For a different kind of problem, consider the idea of largeness. Anything large will participate in the idea of largeness in some sense. Does that mean that there is a small part of the idea of largeness in each large thing? But how can one have a small bit of largeness? The objections continue to mount up, calling into question the whole coherence of a theory of ideal forms. The thing to remember, though, is that it is Plato himself who is raising these objections. He had tentatively put forward a solution to a series of complex metaphysical problems and now, in the *Parmenides*, he subjects that tentative solution to rigorous cross-examination.

One of the most interesting and well-known arguments in the *Parmenides* against ideal forms is known as 'the third man argument'. It goes like this. One of the things the theory of forms is supposed to do is to explain how it is that multiple objects share the same characteristics. The ideal form of horse stands over and above all the particular examples of real horses as it is the point of reference by which their similarities are explained. But, as Plato has Parmenides object, surely one would then need a further ideal form of horse to explain what the particular horses and the first ideal form have in common, and so on again, ad infinitum. This argument does not just appear in Plato's *Parmenides*. It can also be found in the fragments of an early work by Aristotle called *On Ideas*, perhaps written when he was still a student at the Academy. In Aristotle's version, the example used is the ideal form of man. There will be a plurality of individual men and an ideal form of man to explain what those men have in common. But one will then need a third man to explain what the individual men and the ideal form have in common, and a fourth, and a fifth, and so on.

We might wonder who came up with this objection first, Plato or Aristotle? Neither Plato's *Parmenides* nor Aristotle's

On Ideas can be dated precisely, so we cannot know for sure. One view presents Aristotle as the brilliant precocious student who demolished his master's cherished theory. Did he write it up first, only for Plato to take up the objection later? In the *Parmenides*, Plato mentions an Aristotle a number of times, although because the dialogue is set in the previous century it is clearly not intended to be our Aristotle. But could this nevertheless be a jokey reference to the brilliant young student who formulated some of the dialogue's objections? We cannot know one way or the other.

All of what we have seen so far gives us a sense of the intellectual climate in the Academy at the time that Aristotle was a student. There were no doubt vigorous debates about these highly abstract questions concerned with what truly exists, what it is possible to know, and what it means to say that something *is*. Plato's own earlier attempts to answer these questions were subjected to close examination and criticism. If Aristotle wasn't the precocious young genius who dismantled his teacher's most famous theory, then he was at the very least a contributor to collaborative discussions led by Plato in which members of the Academy grappled with these complex metaphysical questions.

Aristotle's own approach to these sorts of questions in his *Metaphysics* can be seen as a continual struggle with the ideas of Plato. He was both a strident critic of his old teacher while also remaining deeply influenced by him. There are many extended attacks on Plato's theory of ideal forms in Aristotle's book, along with criticisms of all his other philosophical predecessors. But Aristotle does not merely define his project in opposition to others; he has his own guiding questions.

In the *Metaphysics*, Aristotle says that he is primarily concerned with the study of being 'in so far as it is being'. In the case of a horse, we can think of it as a horse, more generally as an animal, as an example of a living thing, or simply as something that exists. What is something when understood simply in terms of its *is*-ness? This sounds as if it shares something in common with Parmenides' way of thinking, and it does. But one of the first things that Aristotle insists on is thinking further about what it means to say that something *is*. As he puts it, 'being is said in many ways'. Parmenides only said it in one way – either something *is* or *is not* – and perhaps that is why he ended up with such counter-intuitive conclusions. Aristotle suggested that instead we ought to think about the variety of ways in which we can say that something *is*. For instance, we can say simply that an acorn *is*, which is to say that it is an existing thing, a being. The Greek word that Aristotle used is *ousia*, literally 'being'. Traditionally this has been translated as 'substance', and so any existing thing is referred to as a substance. We can also say that an acorn *is* brown. The brownness isn't an essential property of the acorn, because we can conceive of acorns that aren't brown, so the brownness is what we might call an 'accidental property'. It exists, but it does so in a way that is different from the way in which the acorn itself exists. The acorn itself is a substance, because it exists in its own right; the brownness exists in a different way, because it is merely a feature of a substance. Brownness only exists as an attribute of substances, in this case, the acorn. As we can see, this is in effect the reverse of Plato's theory of forms. Plato would have argued that the ideal form of brownness is the thing that truly exists, along with the ideal form of acorn. Particular acorns are mere copies of the ideal form. For Aristotle, it's the actual acorns that are primary substances, the things that properly exist.

This idea is developed further in another of Aristotle's works, the *Categories*. There he draws a distinction between what he calls 'primary' and 'secondary' substances. Primary substances are actually existing things, like the acorn, a horse, or you, or me. Secondary substances include species, such as human being. There's a sense in which primary substances – you and me as particular humans – are also within the secondary substance of the species human being. We fall within that group or type. Like 'brown', 'human being' is something that we can say about a thing. The reason why primary substances – actually existing particular things – are primary is because none of these other things can exist without them. If there were no human beings, there would be no species called human being. As Aristotle puts it, 'if the primary substances did not exist it would be impossible for any of the other things to exist'. In this sense, they underlie all other things. The colour brown does not exist in the abstract; it only exists because brown things exist.

It seems fairly clear that this too reverses Plato's theory. The colour brown and the species human being do not exist apart from the particular examples to which they belong. Even so, we are told that human being is a secondary *substance*, and that sounds, well, like something substantial, like something that really exists. Is this a residual influence from Plato's theory of ideal forms, still assuming that the concept of human being has some kind of independent existence? Perhaps this is just a matter of translation.

The English word 'substance' is used to translate Aristotle's *ousia*, 'being', because in the early sixth century AD the philosopher Boethius used *substantia* to translate *ousia* in his Latin version of the *Categories* and this became the standard translation throughout the Middle Ages. It's a good translation when talking about what Aristotle here calls 'primary substances', because it has connotations of something underlying, a substrate. But perhaps it's misleading when we are talking about other things. Perhaps we should say that the species human being 'exists secondarily' rather than being a 'secondary substance'. Indeed, at one point, Aristotle himself says that strictly speaking only primary substances ought to be called substances, so he himself was aware of the potential confusion here – suggesting that this is not merely a problem of translation. Later he is even more emphatic, stating that the language of substance may make it sound as if the species or idea of human being exists as a singular thing (like a Platonic ideal form), but this is not the case, for it is merely a quality of particular humans. But even so, he does want to insist that species like human being or horse, or wider classifications such as animal or plant, are real things. They do genuinely exist. They are not merely labels that we have created by noticing some similarities between particular objects; they reflect the objective structures of the natural world. Not only that, they are also essential for understanding particular objects. For instance, whether someone is tall or short, overweight or slender, is merely accidental to who they are and is subject to change, whereas the fact that they are a human being is fundamental to what they are; it is their defining characteristic. We cannot understand what a particular human being is without reference to the fact that they are indeed a human being.

But let's return to our acorn. It is a primary substance and, as such, can be the bearer of various attributes, such as brownness. There's something else we can say about the acorn too. An acorn is not merely an acorn; it is also something that can grow into an oak tree. It is, Aristotle would say, *potentially* an oak tree. Indeed, one might say that if someone is to have any idea about what an acorn really is, they will have to know that it is something that can grow into a tree. If someone didn't know that, they would have no idea what they had in front of them, even though they could see what it was and that it was small, brown, and so on. So, this is another way in which we can say that something *is*, although initially it seems a bit paradoxical, because we are also saying what it *is not*. The acorn is not an oak tree, at least not at the moment, but at the same time it is potentially an oak tree. Not only is it potentially an oak tree, but the fact that it is able to grow into an oak tree is in a sense its essential defining characteristic. What it currently *is not*, defines what it *is*. This is one of the ways in which Aristotle breaks through Parmenides' claim that something either *is* or *is not*.

That gives us three ways in which something can be: as a substance (the acorn), as an attribute or property of a substance (brownness), and as a potentiality (the not yet existent oak tree). 'Being' can be said in many ways. The last of these introduces a key conceptual distinction in Aristotle's philosophy: the difference between actuality and potentiality. Everything that exists is actually something right now and potentially something else, through a process of change. These potentialities are not vague, hypothetical possibilities; they are closely tied to the essence of a thing, like the acorn and the oak tree. (The word 'essence' is another way to translate *ousia*, the being or substance of a thing.) But there are different senses in which something can be actual or potential. The acorn has the potential to become a tree; it is something that it may become in the future. That's one sense of potentiality. But what about an animal which has the potential to move, even though at present it might be lying down? If the animal does get up and move, it does not become something different or change in any dramatic way. Instead, it simply uses a capacity that it has, the ability to move. When we talk of people not fulfilling their potential, we often use the term in this second sense: they had certain capacities or abilities, but they failed to use them. But we also use it in the first sense too, such as when someone notices something in a child, a spark of talent, and comments that they might have the potential to develop into a successful athlete or musician or whatever it may be. When we talk in these ways, we are using technical concepts first developed by Aristotle.

This idea of using an ability or capacity is also central to Aristotle's thinking about what it means to be something. What is a human being? It's a creature of a certain size and shape, usually with two arms and two legs, and so on. But a human being is not merely an object; it is a living thing and a living thing is defined by the capacities and abilities that it has. It's these capacities which distinguish a living human being from a corpse. So, a human being is a living thing with a certain set of capacities: the ability to grow, move, and reproduce. These capacities are ones that we share with other animals. The distinctive capacity of humans, Aristotle says, is the ability to reason: humans are rational animals. The defining characteristic of humans, then, is the ability to think rationally. The vast majority of adult humans have this capacity; we are all, we might say, potentially thinking beings. However, we are only truly thinking beings when we are actually thinking, when we actualize that potential and use the capacity. In short, to *be* a human being is not to exist statically, but instead to engage in a whole range of distinctively human activities, the most important of which is thinking.

'Being' is indeed said in many ways. This last idea of being as activity – a thing *using* its abilities or capacities – is starkly at odds with Parmenides' and Plato's insistence that the only things that truly exist are things that are unchanging. Yet Aristotle did not completely reject that idea either, and in his *Metaphysics* he considered what sorts of things, if any, could be unchanging and eternal. He thought that something must be. The natural world is full of moving bodies, growing and decaying – change is everywhere. But the idea of all this movement suddenly starting at some point, without cause, just seemed nonsensical. Aristotle took heed of Parmenides' argument that something cannot come to be out of nothing. There must be some kind of first cause, underpinning all this natural movement, but not a first cause in the sense of the earliest in a long chain of causes and effects, which would have to come out of nothing. Instead, what he had in mind was something else: something always, eternally moving, some ever-present source of activity. What could that possibly be? In search of an answer, Aristotle simply looked up: the heavens. Stars and planets revolve around the earth (or so he and everyone else thought at the time) and they keep doing so in regular and continuous motion. Aristotle's claim that the heavens are eternal and unchanging was not a mere assumption; it was based on his knowledge of ancient Babylonian and Egyptian astronomical records which charted these regular movements. Aristotle's commentator Simplicius, writing in the sixth century AD, claimed that these records stretched back over a million years. Although we might know better now, Aristotle was following the best evidence available to him at the time.

We are beginning to get a sense of Aristotle's intense curiosity about these sorts of fundamental questions, a curiosity that he was no doubt born with, but which was encouraged and fed during his time at Plato's Academy. All of us by nature desire to know, he said. It is perfectly natural for us to ask these sorts of questions; indeed, it is part of what makes us who we are. Humans are rational animals and reason is our distinctive capacity. In order to be human in the full sense, we must not merely *have* this capacity but also *use* it. At the highest level, that means reflecting about these sorts of metaphysical questions. Aristotle developed these ideas further in his *Nicomachean Ethics*, in which he reflected on what the ideal life for a human being might look like. He considered a number of candidates but only two looked plausible. Let's call the first 'the contemplative life': a life entirely devoted to intellectual inquiry, but one that overlooks the fact that we are embodied social animals with physical needs. It is the life of someone lost in abstract speculation, often at the cost of everything else. Think of the brilliant but absent-minded professor who is an expert in their field but is unable to handle their daily affairs or – perhaps to be more accurate – is completely uninterested in such trivial matters because they have better things to think about. This sort of person is nothing new: an anecdote reported by Plato recounts how the early Greek philosopher Thales of Miletus (Aristotle calls him one of the first philosophers) was once so absorbed looking up and studying the stars that he fell into a well; a passing girl mocked him, saying that while he might know the movements of the heavens he didn't know what was directly under his feet. This became a popular trope and the story of the absent-minded astronomer appears in Aesop's *Fables*.

Is this really the best way for a human being to live? Perhaps, Aristotle comments, it is 'too high' for us. It would be the ideal life for a purely rational being, a pure intellect, but that's not what we are. It is the best form of life for the best part of us, we might say, but perhaps not wholly suitable when we consider ourselves as embodied human beings. Or perhaps it is a way of life suitable for only a handful of people in society, not all. It's no doubt a good thing that there are a few absent-minded professors in the world, but a society composed solely of such people would soon collapse. Even so, there seems little doubt that this is what Aristotle himself aspired to, and that he thought all of us should aspire to it as well, at least in part, or from time to time. To reflect on these big, fundamental questions, to think about the nature of being and to contemplate the order and structure of the heavens, is part of what it means to be human. There's no higher activity to which we can devote our time.

CHAPTER 2
Studying Nature

Questions about the nature of being are the highest and most abstract ones that people can ask. While Aristotle thought that these sorts of questions were at the pinnacle of human inquiry, he was equally interested in countless others lower down the scale. As we have seen, his *Physics* was placed before the *Metaphysics* in the early catalogue of his works and in it Aristotle explored a wide range of questions about the changing natural world. For him, the key difference between these two areas of study is that while metaphysics deals with what *is* (i.e. unchanging), physics deals with what is *going to be* (i.e. changing). Physics is the study of the natural world and nature is primarily a series of processes. In the *Physics*, Aristotle tackles the most basic, fundamental questions connected to the study of nature, from causation, location, and time, through to divisibility and infinity. As well as these general reflections on nature as a whole, Aristotle was also interested in the nitty-gritty details of how nature works. In particular, he was interested in trying to understand living beings – animals – because these are parts of nature that not only move and change but are able to move and change themselves. These interests came to the fore in the period after Aristotle left the Academy.

Aristotle had been in Athens at the Academy for twenty

years when Plato died in 347 BC. Control of the Academy passed to Plato's nephew, Speusippus. This has sometimes been seen as an unfair act of nepotism, for surely Aristotle was Plato's most brilliant student and deserved to be his successor as head of the school. The real reason, however, might have had more to do with the transfer of ownership of property. As an outsider, Aristotle was not an Athenian citizen and so was not allowed to own property; there may have also been pressure to keep such an asset within the family. Either way, it seemed like a good time for Aristotle to move on. During his time in Athens, Aristotle had become friends with Hermias, who was destined to become the ruler of Assos, a city on the coast of Asia Minor. Aristotle decided to follow Hermias there and, not long after, married his niece, Pythias. Aristotle stayed in Assos for around three years, before moving to the nearby island of Lesbos.

Aristotle's time spent on Lesbos was pivotal for his intellectual development. The island was the home of Theophrastus, a native of the city of Eresus, who would become Aristotle's lifelong friend and collaborator. It is not clear if Aristotle already knew Theophrastus before moving to Lesbos. One report suggests that Theophrastus had spent time at the Academy, so perhaps they knew each other already. He may have been part of the small group that left the Academy with Aristotle and headed to Assos. Perhaps it was Theophrastus who suggested that they move on to Lesbos, his old home. Or maybe Aristotle met him on the island for the first time, after he had arrived. We don't know the details, but we do know that Theophrastus would become a key figure throughout the rest of Aristotle's life.

On Lesbos, Aristotle threw himself into the study of nature

and, in particular, the study of animals. On the southern coast, there is an opening into a lagoon, a large body of water in the centre of the island, and this was where Aristotle spent his days. In particular, he studied the marine life of the lagoon and, based on his descriptions, it is clear that he devoted some of his time to dissecting animals. As just one example among many, consider the following from his *History of Animals*:

> The crayfish . . . has two teeth, large and hollow . . . and in between the teeth is a fleshy substance, shaped like a tongue. After the mouth comes a short oesophagus, and then a membranous stomach attached to the oesophagus, and at the orifice of the stomach are three teeth . . . Coming off obliquely from the stomach is a gut, simple and of equal thickness throughout the entire length of the body until it reaches the anal vent.

Elsewhere he compares the inner workings of the cuttlefish and the octopus. He'd clearly examined both carefully. On the basis of these close studies and dissections, Aristotle set about classifying these animals and many more into different genera and species. He gained an understanding of the animal world beyond anything that anyone had achieved before.

There were of course limits to how much Aristotle could know. In his work *Generation of Animals*, Aristotle tried to explain the reproduction of bees. He opens his account by frankly acknowledging that it is a great puzzle. He doesn't really know. Even so, he tackles the question by going through all the different logical possibilities: they generate offspring themselves, they go and get them from somewhere else, or a combination of both. He then considers all the different possible ways in which different types of bees might combine to mate. Although he doesn't know how the process works, he nevertheless manages to map out all the possible explanatory options and tries to rule out the least likely. The most interesting part, however, is his final comment: 'the facts have not been sufficiently ascertained; if at any future time they are ascertained, then credence must be given to the direct evidence of the senses more than to theories'. At some points in his works on animals, Aristotle seems to entertain some fairly wild hypotheses – that some animals spontaneously generate, for instance – but this remark makes clear that these should be taken as no more than educated guesses until the truth can be uncovered through further observation.

Aristotle clearly loved this work, even if it might appear to others as messy and trivial. After all, many of his philosophical predecessors had spent their time not skulking around in mud and marshes but contemplating the eternal heavens and developing complex theories about the origins of the cosmos. But Aristotle was unapologetic, commenting that 'in all natural things there is something marvellous'. He took joy from his study of animals and insects and thought it was odd that people would devote so much time to the study of art, which produced mere representations of natural things, but turn away from the beauty of the natural world itself. His own ambitions as a 'student of nature' were all-encompassing, from the heavens, through meteorological phenomena of the skies, down to the smallest animals and plants. He never managed to study plants in detail, but this task was taken up by Theophrastus, whose works on botany stand shoulder to shoulder with Aristotle's own works on zoology.

Aristotle's writings about animals make up over a quarter of his total surviving works. We have his *History of Animals*, *Generation of Animals*, *Parts of Animals*, *Movement of Animals*, and *Progression of Animals*. It is only fairly recently that scholars have started to pay close attention to these works. They are clearly significant simply in terms of their volume, but they also shed important light on the rest of Aristotle's philosophy. It was through his close study of animals that Aristotle developed his own notion of form, to replace Plato's account of ideal forms.

As we have already seen, Plato conceived forms as unchanging and independently existing entities that function as models for particular instances of a thing, which are mere shadows or copies of the form itself. There is an immaterial idea of horse, and every actually existing horse in the physical world is in some sense a copy of this, or participates in this in some way. The precise relationship is unclear, even to Plato himself, who tried to work through a number of different accounts in his dialogues with only limited success. In contrast to this, as we have also seen, for Aristotle the form or species of horse exists within particular horses: if there were no horses, there would be no independently existing form of horse.

But what do we mean by 'form'? And in what sense does a form exist *within* an object? One of Plato's problems was trying to make sense of how an immaterial idea could be within a physical object, or how that immaterial idea could be present in multiple physical objects. In his discussions, Plato used two Greek words, more or less interchangeably, *idea* and *eidos*. Unsurprisingly, the English 'idea' comes from the Greek word *idea*. It is the Greek word *eidos* which is usually translated as 'form'. One of the central meanings of *eidos* is 'shape'. A horse is a horse, as opposed to any other kind of animal, because it has the shape of a horse. By 'shape' here we needn't mean merely external appearance; we can use it to refer to the structure and organization of the matter that makes up the horse, both inside and out. It has to have all the right parts in all the right places. This, then, is a preliminary meaning of 'form'. As we can see, it is not something *in* the horse, in the sense of being a component alongside the matter out of which it is made. Instead, it is the way in which that matter is ordered and arranged.

That, however, cannot be the whole story. When Aristotle was dissecting fish on the shore of the lagoon in Lesbos, examining in detail the internal structure and organization of the matter that made up these creatures, he was all too conscious of one thing: these animals were dead. Something quite literally vital was missing. As he commented, 'a corpse has the same shape and structure as a living body, and yet it is not a human being'. Similarly, a sculpture of a hand made out of wood or bronze is not a real hand, even if it shares the same shape. What's missing? Aristotle points out that a corpse or a statue, although it might have the shape of a human being, cannot perform the *functions* of a human being. It cannot do the things that humans do. (We are back to the idea of 'being' involving activity.) The same applies to all the individual parts of a thing. What is an eye? It is something that can see. We might say that its function is sight. There's a sense in which the eye in a corpse is no longer really an eye at all, because it can no longer see; it has lost its function. For Aristotle, then, the notion of form covers not merely the shape and structure of a thing, but also – indeed, primarily – its function. These two things are obviously closely interrelated. In order to be able to work in a specific way, all the parts need to be arranged appropriately. But, as we can see from the example of the corpse, they are not identical. If you want to understand what a human or a horse or a fish is, what you need to know first and foremost is that these are *living* animals, capable of doing things. They have functions, capacities, abilities.

While in one sense Aristotle's account of form was a departure from Plato's, there was still much in common. Plato too had considered the importance of function in his *Republic*, where he argued that the definition of something being good is that it fulfils its function. A good knife is one that cuts; a good eye is one that can see. Aristotle's real target was not his old teacher but another philosopher, who had offered a quite different explanation of how nature works: Democritus. Like Aristotle, Democritus was originally from northern Greece – his home city of Abdera was not too far from Aristotle's birthplace, Stagira. He was roughly contemporary with Socrates and is remembered first and foremost for his contributions to the theory of atomism. According to this theory, everything in the physical world is made out of atoms, tiny bits of indestructible matter that move around within an infinite void, randomly colliding with each other, and sometimes sticking to each other, in the process forming the larger visible objects that we can see and touch. Everything, Democritus claimed, can be explained solely in terms of the movements of these tiny bits of matter. If we want to understand what something is, we simply break it down into its constituent parts. But Aristotle knew from his study of animals at Lesbos that this simply wasn't the case. He had cut up his fish, taken them apart, and looked carefully at the matter out of which they were made. He had all the parts laid out before him. However, this didn't really tell him anything about the true nature of the animal as a living being. Even having all the parts together in the appropriate places before full dissection didn't help him understand the *living* creature. For that, one needed to understand its function.

Aristotle rejected what we might call 'reductive materialism': the idea that we can explain something simply in terms of its material components. But he also rejected the idea that anything exists over and above actual physical things. As we have already seen, for him the things that most fully exist are primary substances: this fish, this horse, this human being. These things are, we might say, a combination of form and matter, although 'combination' might make it sound as if form were some kind of component or part alongside the matter, which would be misleading. Aristotle's position is often called 'hylomorphism', from the Greek words for matter (*hylē*) and form or shape (*morphē*). Everything that exists as a primary substance is a physical thing made out of matter, but it's the form that is key to understanding what it is:

> If we were describing a bed or any other like article, we should endeavour to describe the form of it rather than the matter – or, at any rate, the matter, if described, would be described as belonging to the concrete whole. For example,

a bed is a certain form in certain matter, or, alternatively, certain matter that has a certain form, so we should have to include its shape and the manner of its form in our description of it – because the formal nature is of more fundamental importance than the material nature.

The distinction between the form or shape of the bed and the matter out of which it is made is fairly straightforward. To that we can add that the bed also has a specific function or purpose – it is a piece of furniture designed to be slept on – and so both the form and the matter have to be suitable in order for it to achieve that. After all, a bed that does not fulfil the purpose of a bed is no bed at all. Something might superficially look like a bed, but if you can't sleep on it, then it's not really a bed. But this is a fairly simple example, because a bed is an inert thing. For reductive materialists like Democritus, the matter out of which all things are made is dead and inert. If that were the case, one might wonder how it is that some things are alive. One can imagine Aristotle thinking just this as he examined the dissected parts of a fish. How is it that when all these material components are put together the resulting combination is a living thing that can move by itself? But as we've seen, for Aristotle these material components are not the primary building blocks of nature. For him, nature consists of primary substances – fish, horses, human beings – and these particular examples are all living organisms. While there is much in the natural world that isn't alive – rocks and dirt and water – it's the living organism that presents the greatest challenge to anyone trying to understand nature. These are the things that we need to be able to explain. The challenge is to grasp the complexity of the living animal, not to reduce it to a pile of dust.

What is it that makes something alive? What distinguishes a living being from a corpse? The Greeks had a word for this: *psychē*. The *psychē* is whatever it is that animates a living being and is gone when it is dead. All living things have *psychē*, including plants. It is traditionally translated as 'soul', although that has perhaps unhelpful religious connotations and is probably too narrow in meaning (but, as is common practice, we'll stick with it here). It is the principle of life, the thing that makes things alive. In his work *Parts of Animals*, Aristotle wrote that 'it may be that the form of any living creature is soul', adding that 'when its soul is gone, it is no longer a living creature'. This led him to conclude that understanding the nature of soul ought to be a central concern for any student of nature.

Let's think for a moment about this idea that soul might be the form of a living creature. As we saw earlier, for Aristotle 'form' has to mean more than just shape, structure, or the organization of matter, because that wouldn't explain the difference between a living being and a corpse. Their structures are identical, yet they are decidedly different. What distinguishes them? A living being can *do* things, it can use its capacities and abilities. The form of a living being, then, must involve this idea of capacities or functions. These are what make it alive. If 'soul' refers to whatever it is that makes something alive – whatever distinguishes a living being from a corpse – then it looks as if we ought to understand 'soul' as a set of capacities and abilities. So, we can identify the soul of a living being with its form, which as we have just seen is defined in the same way. As Aristotle put it in the opening lines of his work devoted to the topic, *On the Soul* (usually referred to by its Latin title, *De Anima*), 'the soul is as it were the first principle of animal life'.

In *De Anima*, Aristotle starts by drawing on some of the questions he asked when thinking about the nature of being. If the soul exists, then in what sense does it exist? Is it a thing, a substance? Is it merely a quality or attribute of some other substance? Does it exist actually or potentially? Reflecting on his time spent studying animals on Lesbos, he comments that when most people ask these questions they are only really thinking about the human soul. But Aristotle is interested in the souls of all living things, including whether they all share the same type of soul. How, if at all, does the soul of a dog differ from that of a human being? How does the soul relate to the body? In answer to the last question, Aristotle is quick to assert that the soul is closely tied to the body. For a start, we never encounter one apart from a body; second, many of the emotions that we attribute to the soul – anger, fear, love – all have a bodily component. Our emotional lives are intensely physical: we get hot and bothered, we blush, we turn pale, we become tense. That might lead us to think that the soul is itself something material, a component in the body governing it, but we already have a sense that Aristotle will reject that option.

Earlier we saw him draw a distinction between two types of actuality and potentiality. We have the 'actuality of speech' in one sense when we are actually talking, but we have it in another sense when we have the capacity for speech but are not using it right now. I am a speaking being even when I'm silent, in a way that, say, a dog is not. Both the dog and I are currently not saying anything, but nevertheless I have the 'actuality of speech' in the sense of having the capacity. Aristotle says that the soul is like this, because it exists even when we are not using all its capacities, such as when we are asleep. Aristotle's formal definition, in his characteristically precise but opaque style, is that 'the soul is the first actuality of a natural body which has life potentially'. Thankfully, Aristotle is also very good at illustrating his points with intuitive examples. When thinking about the relationship between soul and body – or any combination of form and matter – we ought to think of it like the relationship between an impression in a piece of wax and the wax in which it has been made. The impression clearly cannot exist without the wax. At the same time, the wax must be shaped in some way. Another favourite example is a bronze statue of a figure. The figure cannot exist without the bronze, and the bronze always has to have some kind of shape. Form and matter always exist together: hylomorphism. But these examples focus on shape, not function, so Aristotle considers another: an axe. If we were to ask what the essence or being of an axe is, it would be 'what it is to be an axe, [and] this would be its soul'. And the essence of an axe is the ability to cut wood. The essence of an eye is the ability to see, so Aristotle says that if the eye were an animal, its soul would be sight. For a living being, its essence is life. In the case of plants, the defining characteristic is the ability to take in nourishment and grow. With animals, there is not only this capacity but also the ability to perceive and to move. Humans have all these capacities along with the ability to think. For us humans, the soul is that by which we live, perceive, and think.

The soul – these abilities – is our essence, our defining char-acteristic. But Aristotle will also insist that we are not merely our souls; we are primarily embodied living animals.

So far, we've considered form and matter as two things that help to explain existing things, substances. If we want to understand anything in the natural world, both of these will have to feature in our account or explanation of it. I cannot give an adequate account of any physical object without saying what it is made out of and how that stuff is arranged and structured. So, matter and form are going to be two key parts of any description. Aristotle calls these *aitiai*, which has the sense of 'explanations', 'reasons', or 'causes'. Although 'ex-planations' is probably the most helpful way to think about them, traditionally they have been called 'causes'. Form and matter – or the formal and material causes – are in fact just two out of four causes that Aristotle thinks are essential for a proper understanding of anything. His account of these four causes reappears throughout his works; it can be found in his *Physics* and he repeats it in his works on animals too. So, what are the other two causes? The first of these is a cause in the usual English sense of that word, as when we say that a push caused a ball to move. This is often referred to as an 'efficient cause'. The second is more interesting and, for Aristotle, the most important of them all: the 'final cause'. This is the goal or purpose at work in any given process. If something hap-pens, and we ask why, the answer to that question will be the final cause, the 'that for the sake of which' it happened. For example, if we see someone putting bricks on top of one an-other, and we want to understand what's going on, we'll need to refer to all four of the causes or parts of explanation: the fact that they are bricks (the matter), the way in which they are being arranged (the form), what it is that is making this happen (the builder, as the efficient cause), and *why* it is happening, which in this case is in order to build a wall. Aristotle's key thought here is that in order really to understand what is going on at all, we need to know that someone is trying to build a wall: we need to know what the process is aiming at, what its goal is. An explanation that leaves this out is no explanation at all. This is another point where Aristotle questions the reductive materialism of people like Democritus. An explanation which tries to explain the natural world simply by referring to the movement of material components like atoms doesn't really explain anything, Aristotle would say. We need to know the *why*; we need to know where the process is heading.

In the case of someone building a wall, the fact that there's a final goal or purpose comes as no great surprise. The builder is a conscious agent who has a plan of what he is trying to do and so his actions are intentional. As Aristotle himself puts it, 'the builder sets before himself something quite definite', and on the basis of this he can tell you why he is doing what he does. But what about natural processes? Can there be similar intentions and purposes in nature? Aristotle was adamant that there are, insisting that the final cause is 'more fully present in the works of nature than in the works of art and craft'. In claiming this, he was arguing against previous thinkers who had claimed that things come to be as they are simply through chance. Once again, Democritus was a target, but Aristotle also had in mind another earlier philosopher, called Empedocles. Empedocles had claimed that the seemingly designed features of animals were in fact the product of chance and random mutations. In effect, Empedocles proposed a theory of evolution. (Earlier still, Anaximander had suggested that the first animals to exist were fish, out of which humans developed.) Potentially embarrassingly, Aristotle dismissed Empedocles' early attempt at evolutionary theory out of hand. It was preposterous, he thought, to claim that nature was random and that the structures of organisms were the product of chance. A horse has the features that it does because its parents were horses. Its nature is predetermined by what it has inherited from its parents. This inheritance is passed on via the seed (in Greek, *sperma*) that created it. What's passed on is information about how the new animal ought to grow. In Aristotle's terms, this is the form, transmitted from parent to offspring. The seed of one kind of animal only ever produces the same kind of animal: dogs produce dogs, never cats. Even if he might have rejected evolutionary theory, Aristotle had (pun intended) an embryonic idea of DNA.

Assessing Aristotle's work on animals, the biologist Armand Marie Leroi made the following observations about the four causes. The efficient cause, he commented, 'is an account of the mechanics of movement and change. It is now the domain of developmental biology and neurophysiology. The material cause is an account of the matter – the stuff – of which animals are made, and their properties. It is now the domain of modern biochemistry and physiology.' So far so good. But what about the formal and final causes? Leroi continues: 'The formal cause is an account of the information transmitted that any creature received from its parents, and that is responsible for the features that it shares with other members of its species – that is, the subject matter of genetics. The final cause is teleology, the analysis of the parts of animals in terms of their functions. It is now the part of evolutionary biology that studies adaptation.' Although Aristotle's biology has inevitably been left far behind by developments in science since, his core insights into how best to try to understand nature still ring true today. All four of these types of explanation are parts of a modern scientific explanation of life.

The idea that processes have some aim or goal is closely related to the idea that things have a function. Earlier we said that the function of an eye is to see; now we might say that the eye is *for* seeing, that's its goal or purpose. Sometimes, these causes coincide, especially the formal and final causes. Consider the process by which animals reproduce; let's say a new horse is being born. The material cause is the stuff out of which it is made. The efficient cause will be the parents, horses. The formal cause – explaining what this new creature is – will be the form of a horse. The final cause – what the process is for – is to produce a new horse. There's a sense in which 'horse' answers the question for three out of the four causes.

One of the things that Aristotle learned from his study and dissection of animals was that each organ within an organism served some purpose for the organism as a whole. The purpose of the eye is to see, the heart to pump blood, the lungs to breathe, and so on. They all play their part in sustaining the organism. But what about the organism itself? Does that have a purpose or goal? What, if anything, are animals for? Aristotle asked himself this question, commenting that 'the body as a whole must exist for the sake of some complex action'. His answer was 'the body exists for the sake of the soul'. Given that, as we have seen, soul was defined as 'that which makes us alive', his answer is in effect that the organism's goal is simply to live its appropriate form of life. All the different complex parts of the organism contribute to that end. And, as Aristotle said earlier, there's a sense in which this goal – i.e. the final cause – is the key to any attempt to understand a living thing. If you are trying to understand the behaviour of plants, animals, or humans – from photosynthesis to nest-building to advanced technology – you need to know what it is for, and ultimately it is for survival, to sustain its way of life.

The goal of organisms in general, then, is to be alive – to survive and to reproduce. What about the goal of human beings in particular? Aristotle asks himself this question in his *Nicomachean Ethics*. His aim there is to try to work out what a good life for a human being might look like. Given that humans are just another type of animal, he approaches this question in part with his biologist's hat on. First, iden-tify the function specific to human beings. This will tell us what the most appropriate activities for a human will be. A good human being will be one that fulfils that function, and a good life will be one marked by the corresponding activ-ity. So, what's the specific function of human beings? It is not merely to stay alive, which is something we share with all other ensouled beings, including plants. Nor is it just to use our senses and move around, which we share with other animals. The distinctive human ability that sets us apart is our rationality. As Aristotle puts it, 'the function of human beings is activity of the soul in accordance with reason'.

Aristotle thus draws on his research into animals to help

him understand us as humans – one animal among many – and to offer an answer to the question of how we ought to live. His answer is simple: we ought to use our reason, our distinctive capacity, in order to try to understand the world around us, just as he did. It is important to stress *use* our reason: we are talking here about actualizing a potential, making use of a capacity, engaging in an activity, devoting our time to trying to understand ourselves and the world in which we live.

CHAPTER 3
A Rational Animal

In his attempt to identify a function for human beings, Aristotle suggested that we are distinctively rational animals. It is reason that separates us from other creatures. The Greek word translated here as 'reason' is *logos*, a broad term which can mean many things. In this context it means reason, but it can also mean 'word', 'account', 'explanation', or 'something said'. It is a noun derived from the verb *legein*, 'to say' or 'to speak'. Humans are the only animals that can talk, that can offer verbal explanations of things, and engaging in complex verbal communication inevitably requires a degree of rationality or intelligence. So, when Aristotle points to *logos* as the uniquely human feature that separates us from other animals, he is referring to the fact that we can think, talk, and explain things using complex language. Other animals may well be intelligent in all sorts of ways, and able to communicate with each other, but only humans use language to *explain* things. In this sense, *logos* is unique to us.

Aristotle was fascinated by this ability of ours. It is a distinctively human function, and it's essential that we understand it if we are to know what a good human life is. But it is equally important to understand it if we are to comprehend the world around us: complex scientific knowledge isn't merely a matter of gathering data through observation – it also requires theories built on the back of that data. And we need to be confident that the theories and arguments that we put forward actually work. This led Aristotle to develop a method for assessing arguments and explanations. What counts as a good explanation? When do the conclusions that people draw follow on from the claims that they make? When do our explanations fail? It was in an attempt to respond to these sorts of questions that Aristotle effectively invented logic, the study of *logos*.

Aristotle's logical works were arranged in late antiquity in a specific order as part of a wider teaching curriculum encompassing all of his and Plato's writings. In the early sixth century AD, the Roman senator and philosopher Boethius, whom we met earlier, set out an ambitious plan to translate all the works of Plato and Aristotle into Latin, as well as to write commentaries on them. Unsurprisingly, he failed. But he did manage to translate Aristotle's logical works: the *Categories*, *On Interpretation*, *Prior Analytics*, *Posterior Analytics*, *Topics*, and *Sophistical Refutations*. All these were prefaced by a translation of a short introduction to Aristotle's logic by a philosopher from the third century AD called Porphyry. For the first half of the Middle Ages, these were the only works of Aristotle readily available in Latin Europe. People who knew Aristotle knew him through these works and knew him as, first and foremost, a logician.

Together these logical works were known under the title *Organon*, or 'tool'. This reflected Aristotle's own view that logic was not a part of philosophy proper but instead a tool that we can use when tackling philosophical problems. It teaches us how to argue correctly but it doesn't teach us any substantive truths itself. But that's in no way to diminish the value and importance of logic. On the contrary, whatever topic we might be examining, if we are going to do so effectively, we are going to need to know our logic. That's why from late antiquity onwards it was placed at the very beginning of the curriculum.

The order in which Aristotle's logical works were arranged and taught has sometimes been thought to reflect their contents. The *Categories* effectively dealt with words or terms, so it came first. Then came *On Interpretation*, which dealt with sentences, or, more properly, propositions. The *Prior Analytics* showed how propositions can be joined together to form arguments, or, to use Aristotle's term, syllogisms. Then the *Posterior Analytics* looked at how arguments can be combined to create a more substantial, explanatory body of knowledge. The *Topics* went on to examine a different kind of argument, dialectical reasoning, and the *Sophistical Refutations* – often seen as an appendix to the *Topics* – looked at questionable arguments and fallacies.

However, it is far from clear whether Aristotle had this kind of arrangement in mind or if they were written in this order. There are all sorts of questions about the textual integrity of these works too: the final part of the *Categories*, chapters 10–15, has sometimes been judged not to be by Aristotle at all, or to be a genuine but separate piece of writing tacked on by a later editor. Then there's the question of what these works are really about. In the case of the *Categories*, this itself became a topic of intense debate throughout the Middle Ages. Is it a book about words ('things that are said') or things ('things that are')? Or both? Or something else, such as concepts? If it's a book about words or terms, the building blocks of propositions, then it makes sense to read it as the first step in the traditional logical curriculum. But if it is about things – that is, beings, things that exist – then it is a work of metaphysics, and perhaps not so suitable for beginners. Indeed, one of the longer chapters in the *Categories*, chapter 5, is devoted to the topic of being. For centuries, it was through this passage alone that Latin readers in Europe became acquainted with Aristotle's metaphysical views when the *Metaphysics* was inaccessible.

Because the *Categories* was one of the first works of philosophy that students read, combined with the fact that its subject matter was unclear and that it contained a hefty dose of challenging metaphysics in the middle, this short work by Aristotle became the subject of literally hundreds of commentaries trying to explain its contents. Many of these were significantly longer than the work itself. To give a sense of the challenges it posed – and still poses – to readers, here's the opening chapter:

> Things are said to be named 'equivocally' when, though they have a common name, the definition corresponding with the name differs for each. Thus, a real man and a figure in a picture can both lay claim to the name 'animal'; yet these are equivocally named, for, though they have a common name, the definition corresponding with the name differs for each. For, should anyone define in what sense each is an animal, his definition in the one case will be appropriate to that case only.

On the other hand, things are said to be named 'univocally' which have both the name and the definition answering to the name in common. A man and an ox are both 'animal', and these are univocally named, inasmuch as not only the name, but also the definition, is the same in both cases: for if a man should state in what sense each is an animal, the statement in the one case would be identical with that in the other.

Things are said to be named 'derivatively' which derive their name from some other name, but differ from it in termination. Thus, the grammarian derives his name from the word 'grammar', and the courageous man from the word 'courage'.

Throughout the Middle Ages and beyond, these were the first words by Aristotle that students would have read. The distinctions that he draws here are very useful to know but, even so, it still feels a bit like one is being thrown in at the deep end. Because everyone became familiar with these terms, they came to figure prominently in medieval philosophical debates: when we say that God exists, are we saying so equivocally or univocally? In other words, does God exist in the same sense that physical objects exist (i.e. using the word 'exist' univocally)? If he does, that would seem to imply that he too is something physical. But if he doesn't, if he exists in a completely different sense of 'exist' to the one we know and understand (i.e. equivocally), then can we really comprehend his existence? Neither outcome was acceptable. Without going further into that debate, we can see the way in which medieval theology was carried out using terms and concepts learned from Aristotle.

Here we might think back to Parmenides: something either *is* or *is not*. As we saw earlier, Aristotle's response was to say that 'being' can be said in many ways. In the *Categories*, we get even further distinctions related to how we use words – all of Aristotle's writing is marked by the making of careful distinctions and a desire for precision in language. The categories mentioned in the title are ten different ways in which we can use words. Aristotle says that any word taken on its own can refer to either (1) what something is, i.e. substance; (2) its size and quantity; (3) what sort of thing it is, its quality; (4) its relation to other things; (5) where it is, its location or place; (6) when it is in time; (7) its position; (8) its state or condition; (9) its activity; or (10) what's happening to it. By carefully attending to the different ways in which we use words in different contexts, Aristotle thinks we can avoid some of the confusing and paradoxical claims of earlier philosophers like Parmenides. However, single words don't mean anything on their own. In order to say something – to affirm or deny something – we have to combine them together into sentences or propositions. Because Aristotle is primarily concerned here with what we can know, he is most interested in propositions which make a claim that can be either true or false. Other sentences which don't make such statements are the domain of rhetoric and poetry, which Aristotle examines elsewhere.

If the *Categories* deals with words or terms, then *On Interpretation* might be seen to deal with sentences or propositions. In fact, *On Interpretation* opens by reflecting further on terms before moving on to propositions. It starts by making an important fourfold distinction between (a) written words, which record (b) spoken words, which express (c) thoughts, which reflect (d) things in the world. While written and spoken words can vary between different groups of people, Aristotle insists that the underlying thoughts or concepts, as well as things in the world, are the same for everyone. A word on its own means nothing. Someone can say 'unicorn' (Aristotle's example is *tragelaphos*, 'goat-stag') but this doesn't affirm or deny anything. However, if someone says 'unicorn is' – or, more naturally, 'unicorns exist' – then we have a claim that can be either true or false. We are back to the verb 'to be' again.

Just as the *Categories* classified different types of words, so *On Interpretation* classifies different types of propositions. These can be simple, complex, contradictory, universal, indefinite, affirmative, negative, contrary, and so on. Of all the different types that Aristotle discussed, there was one that really caught the imagination of later commentators. This was his discussion of propositions about the future, and in particular his example 'a sea battle will happen tomorrow'. These sorts of statements were an interesting case for Aristotle, given that he was interested in what we can affirm or deny. If someone were to say 'a sea battle happened yesterday', and one had indeed happened, then their statement would be true. Given that the past is fixed and cannot be changed, Aristotle will say that it is necessary that this statement is true. Nothing can now happen to make it false. The same goes for statements about events happening right now. If a sea battle really is taking place right now, then the statement 'a sea battle is taking place' is without doubt true. But what about statements concerning the future, such as 'a sea battle will happen tomorrow'? Can this be true or false?

Aristotle's concern is this: if all statements or propositions must be either true or false (his opening working assumption), this could lead to the conclusion that everything that happens does so necessarily. If, for instance, someone says 'a sea battle will happen tomorrow', that statement must be either true or false, even if we don't know which. Or let's imagine two people, one who says that it will happen tomorrow and one who says that it won't. One of those two people is speaking the truth. Indeed, we might say that it is necessary that one of their statements is true, even if we don't know which one. If it is necessary now that one is true, then it was equally necessary yesterday that one was true. Yesterday is the past and the past is fixed, so it looks as if the truth of their statement is also fixed. As Aristotle himself puts it, 'someone may predict an event ten thousand years beforehand, and another may predict the reverse; that which was truly predicted at the moment in the past will of necessity take place in the fullness of time'. But, he adds, it doesn't matter whether anyone did actually make these statements in the past. It's not as if someone can magically determine the future just by pronouncing it. What matters is how the world is constructed: 'if through all time the nature of things was so constituted that a prediction about an event was true, then through all time it was necessary that that prediction should find fulfilment'. If the world is constituted in this way, does that mean that the future is predetermined?

Aristotle certainly doesn't think that it is – the future is open and contingent – which is why he's concerned by this conclusion appearing to be a consequence of the seemingly innocuous claim that all statements are either true or false.

As we can see, once we bring time into the equation, things start to get more complicated. What Aristotle is doing here, in effect, is testing his own provisional assumptions to see if they lead to any absurd or contradictory consequences. His challenge here is to reconcile his commitment to the idea that logic generates necessary truths with his view that nature is open and contingent, and that our actions make a difference to the outcome of events.

His solution was to say that the truth of statements depends on *when* they are said. Again, it's useful to hear this in Aristotle's own words, if only to get a fuller sense of his way of thinking:

> What is must be *when* it is, and what is not must not be *when* it is not. Yet it cannot be said without qualification that all existence and non-existence is the outcome of necessity. For there is a difference between saying that what is, *when* it is, must be, and simply saying that what is must be, and similarly in the case of what is not.

Once more, there seems to be an implicit swipe at Parmenides here, who had claimed, without qualification, that what is must be. Aristotle, by contrast, is the master of careful qualification. If I say 'it is daytime', this is not true without qualification, for it depends on *when* I say it, and the same goes for the truthfulness of many other things we say.

The next step on the path to knowledge is to combine statements or propositions into arguments. Philosophers had done this before, of course, but Aristotle's great innovation was to think beyond specific arguments and to reflect, in his *Prior Analytics*, on why it is that some arguments are good and others bad. Why are we convinced by some arguments but not others? Let's take a simple example: all humans are animals; all animals are mortal; therefore, all humans are mortal. It's fairly easy to see that this works. Let's consider another: all humans are animals; all animals can fly; therefore, all humans can fly. We can see that this argument also works, and works in the same way as the first, even though in this case we might doubt the conclusion. We doubt the conclusion because we doubt the statement that 'all animals can fly', which we know not to be true. But Aristotle is not so concerned for the moment with whether particular claims are true or not – those can be settled by observation when he has his scientist's hat on. Instead, he wants to know why these two arguments both work, why it is that the conclusion naturally follows from the first two statements (the premises). In order to study the form or structure of the arguments, he strips out the content to leave it bare. To do this, he replaces the particular terms in the premises with letters of the alphabet. Thus, the first argument becomes 'all As are B; all Bs are C; therefore, all As are C'. The second argument translates into exactly the same, because these two arguments share the same logical form. In both cases, the conclusion follows necessarily from the premises. If the premises are true, then the conclusion will also be true. In the second argument, one of the premises was false, so the conclusion was false, but the argument itself is still what is called valid.

In fact, Aristotle formalized these sorts of arguments slightly differently. He talked of one term being 'predicated' (or said) of another term. When we say 'all animals are mortal', we are predicating 'mortal' of the subject 'animal' – 'mortal' is the predicate. There are a number of different ways in which a term can be predicated of another. A term can be predicated of all or some of another term (all A is B, some A is B), or it can be stated that it is not predicated at all (no A is B) or not predicated of some (some A is not B). Aristotle mapped out all the different possible combinations of three terms into arguments involving two premises and a conclusion. In order for the argument to work, there has to be a 'middle term' which appears in both premises. Working through all the possible permutations, Aristotle identified fourteen valid argument forms, falling into three groups (which he called 'figures'), set out overleaf. This gives a sense of the sort of analytical mind that Aristotle had. It's not just that he worked through all of these logical permutations; he was the very first person even to think about classifying arguments in this way.

Before we move on, there are a couple of things to note about Aristotle's analysis of these arguments. Let's take another example, often repeated: Socrates is a human; all humans are mortal; therefore, Socrates is mortal. This argument differs from the earlier examples because it is about a particular thing, Socrates. He's the subject and the conclusion is about him and him alone. This doesn't fit within the sorts of arguments that Aristotle was interested in, precisely for the reason that it deals with something particular. Scientific knowledge is about making general claims about certain types of things, so that when you come across another instance of the same type you can confidently claim to know things about it already. If you know that *all* humans are mortal, then that tells you something about every new human that you meet. Knowing that this particular human is

A is said of all B;	B is said of all C;	therefore, A is said of all C
A is said of no B;	B is said of all C;	therefore, A is said of no C
A is said of all B;	B is said of some C;	therefore, A is said of some C
A is said of no B;	B is said of some C;	therefore, A is not said of some C

M is said of all N;	M is said of no O;	therefore, N is said of no O
M is said of no N;	M is said of all O;	therefore, N is said of no O
M is said of no N;	M is said of some O;	therefore, N is not said of some O
M is said of all N;	M is not said of some O;	therefore, N is not said of some O

P is said of all S;	R is said of all S;	therefore, P is said of some R
P is said of no S;	R is said of all S;	therefore, P is not said of some R
P is said of some S;	R is said of all S;	therefore, P is said of some R
P is said of all S;	R is said of some S;	therefore, P is said of some R
P is not said of some S;	R is said of all S;	therefore, P is not said of some R
P is said of no S;	R is said of some S;	therefore, P is not said of some R

mortal (in this case, Socrates), doesn't tell you anything that you can apply more widely.

In the traditional order of Aristotle's works, the *Prior Analytics* was – unsurprisingly – followed by the *Posterior Analytics*. This may be a later artificial division, for Aristotle himself simply refers to the *Analytics* as a single work. As we've just seen, the *Prior Analytics* was concerned with the form or structure of arguments, regardless of their content. The goal was to see which argument structures work, which are valid. Whether the premises are true or not was of no concern. 'Some pigs have wings; things with wings can fly; therefore, some pigs can fly.' What mattered was not whether the premises or the conclusion were true, but whether the conclusion followed logically from the premises.

In the *Posterior Analytics*, Aristotle moves forward to consider how we gain knowledge. That does require true premises. Aristotle says that if we have true premises and a valid argument form, then we'll get a true conclusion, a new piece of knowledge. We can also string arguments together into longer chains of reasoning. However, it is important to avoid falling into circular reasoning when doing this; there must be some grounding claims behind the whole chain, which cannot stretch back indefinitely. There must be foundations for our knowledge, whether they be basic axioms in mathematics or confirmed observations in the sciences. If all humans by nature desire to know, here Aristotle is setting out how to go about doing this in a systematic manner.

Both the *Prior* and *Posterior Analytics* examine what Aristotle called 'demonstrative reasoning', the sort that is used in the sciences when they make assertions about how the

world is. In his *Topics* – the next book in the traditional se-
quence of his logical works – Aristotle examines a different
kind of reasoning which would have been all too familiar
from his time at the Academy. Indeed, part of it may have
been written while he was still there. This second type he
calls 'dialectical reasoning'. This is the sort of thing that Socrates used to do in central Athens when he cross-examined
people and, inspired by Socrates' example, it became one of
the central methods in Plato's dialogues. In dialectical reasoning, someone might accept an opening claim or opinion
'for the sake of the argument' and then pursue it wherever it
goes, so that the consequences of that opinion become clear.
This could be done with a great deal of scepticism – someone
might adopt a view which they believe to be false, with the
aim of making explicit its absurd consequences. Equally it
could be used in a sincere search for truth, examining a
potential answer to a problem to see if it stands up.

In the *Topics*, Aristotle suggests that dialectical reasoning
ought to begin from widely held opinions, examining them
to see if they are self-contradictory. He also suggests that, in
the pursuit of knowledge, it can sometimes be useful to argue
both for and against a particular view in order to test it. We can
use this type of reasoning in conversation, accepting someone
else's view even if we might not share it, in order to have a
fruitful discussion. It can also be a valuable form of intellectual
training, such as when teachers ask students to argue for or
against a particular view that the students may not hold themselves. This form of reasoning may be especially useful when
dealing with ethical or political questions – that is, the sorts
of questions that occupied Socrates. It is much easier in the

natural sciences to argue from a secure starting point if there are incontrovertible facts based on observation. But when it comes to questions about, say, what justice is, we are more likely to face a variety of potentially conflicting opinions. Aristotle's approach was to take either widely held opinions or those of prominent individuals and interrogate them to see if they stand up to scrutiny. While he thought that it was possible to come to conclusions when examining issues in ethics and politics, he also acknowledged that trying to answer these sorts of questions is quite different from, say, doing mathematics. It would be foolish, he commented, to look for deductive proofs when discussing ethical problems, just as it would be to think that a mathematician's answers were merely probable.

Aristotle's animal research on Lesbos, involving careful observation and classification, laid some of the foundations for empirical science – but only some. A huge catalogue of information is not on its own enough to generate scientific knowledge. Imagine an old-fashioned museum full of samples of insects or rocks or fossils. Such collections can be fascinating to visit, but on their own they don't really tell us very much. Someone needs to come along and examine all this material, classifying like items with like, but then going further to analyse and reason about all this information, making connections and drawing conclusions. Aristotle was of course already doing this in his biological works, but his works on logic – especially the *Analytics* – take this to the next level, setting out the formal rules for such analysis. In the process, he laid down the remaining foundations for scientific knowledge. To have done either of these would have been a major achievement; to have done both is awe-inspiring.

CHAPTER 4
Social Animals

When he was a young man, Aristotle was not particularly sociable, some accounts suggest. As a student in Plato's Academy, he would have been expected to join in philosophical discussions with his fellow students and perhaps with Plato himself. Inspired by the example of Socrates, Plato saw philosophy as primarily an activity of live debate and discussion – of dialectical reasoning. He tried to capture the spirit of this in his own written dialogues, while at the same time cautioning his readers that written words pale in comparison to a conversation with a real human being. The reason for this, he wrote in his dialogue *Phaedrus*, is simple: one cannot cross-examine words on a page in the way one can a real human being.

It's reported that Aristotle had limited interest in this kind of live philosophical discussion, instead taking himself away to read on his own. He preferred, it seems, the company of books. There are a number of ancient references to his love of books and it is not uncommon to see Aristotle described as one of the world's first book collectors. It seems that he was more interested in learning about the ideas of his predecessors than in arguing with those immediately around him. Indeed, a number of Aristotle's works – *Metaphysics*, *Physics*, *On the Soul* – begin with a survey of the opinions of earlier philosophers culled from Aristotle's reading. This kind of literature review summarizing existing ideas on the topic at hand remains standard practice in academic research to this day. If he were alive now, Aristotle would more likely be the industrious student quietly beavering away in the library than the vocal show-off in the seminar room.

In this sense, then, Aristotle may not have been especially sociable, but in another, deeper sense he certainly saw himself as a social being. In his book devoted to the study of social and political communities, the *Politics*, Aristotle famously described human beings as 'social animals'. The Greek words that he used were *politikon zōion*, and they are sometimes translated as 'political animal'. The adjective *politikon* derives from the noun *polis*. If we were to understand *polis* as 'State', then we might render *politikon* as 'political', but if we take *polis* to mean 'city', then 'social' might be more appropriate; *polis* has connotations of both and is often translated as 'city-state'. The central point Aristotle wanted to make is that by nature human beings live in communities.

Building from the ground up, we see people formed into households and families, motivated by the natural desire to reproduce. A number of these join together to form villages, and this further collaboration enables people to meet more than their basic needs. Finally, villages come together to form a city-state which is large enough to enable people to do far more than merely survive. A city is a community large enough to produce culture – art, theatre, education, philosophy – which is to say that it enables humans not merely to survive but to live a rich, interesting, and good life. That's why, according to Aristotle, the city-state is the ideal political organization. But equally essential to a good life, Aristotle argued, is a sense of involvement in how society is run. In order to actualize our potential as rational agents, we need to be able to make decisions that matter, that contribute to our communities, rather than being passive adherents of rules over which we've had no say. That's why employees in small firms where everyone gets a voice are probably more likely to feel engaged than those in large corporations who are fed instructions via middle managers. We all like to feel part of something and – just as importantly – have a sense of ownership as well. When institutions get too big, the people inside are more likely to become disengaged and feel alienated. That's also what happens when political communities get too big, which is why Aristotle settled on the city-state as the ideal size for a political community: large enough to make the production of culture possible, but still small enough that everyone can play an active role in its operation.

For Aristotle, then, political communities are natural phenomena because humans are social animals. We can contrast this with the typical modern view that sees the State not as something natural but as something created by individuals for the sake of their well-being and protection. The classic statement of this modern view is Thomas Hobbes's famous claim that in the state of nature human life is 'solitary, poore, nasty, brutish, and short'. In order to overcome this, people came together, trading some freedoms for the sake of mutual security. The State is something artificial that we grudgingly accept because it is better than the alternative, a war of all against all. This seems to presuppose that our natural starting point – as unattractive as it may be – is isolated self-interest. Aristotle simply doesn't see this; based on his observations of humans, and no doubt other animals too, it seems self-evident to him that our natural state is one of living with others, in families, tribes, and villages, just as animals live in flocks and herds. After all, humans do not come into existence out of nothing; we are born into families that raise and nurture us. In this sense, the social group comes first and the isolated individual is only ever an aberration from the natural state of living with, and depending on, others.

There is much to admire in Aristotle's account, but also some things that most people today are likely to find troubling. The most obvious of these are his claims that some people can legitimately be described as 'natural slaves' and that women are naturally ruled by men. Unsurprisingly, these claims might lead some people to dismiss Aristotle out of hand, which would be a shame, so they are worth tackling directly. By 'natural slave' he seems to mean someone unable to govern themselves, someone who literally has to depend on the judgements of someone else. By his own criteria, the only people who would fall into this group are those who are mentally impaired in some way – people who have the use of their bodies but not full use of their minds. No one capable of autonomous rational thought could be a slave in his sense. We might draw a parallel with situations when someone manages the affairs of someone else unable to do so for themselves (say, a relative with dementia). That can be an act of kindness, so long as it is done in their best interests. But no one today would want to describe that as slavery.

What we think of as slavery is what Aristotle goes on to call 'legal slavery', such as when previously free individuals are taken as possessions as part of the spoils of war. Aristotle addresses this kind of slavery directly, noting that some people 'hold it to be indefensible that a man who has been overpowered by the violence and superior might of another should become his property'. Aristotle is prepared to acknowledge that there are arguments both for and against this, but his conclusion is fairly clear. He says that a relationship between a master and a slave ought to be mutually beneficial and one of friendship, and it certainly won't be if the relationship 'arises out of the use of force and by the law'. Even so, Aristotle does seem to assume that it is perfectly normal for most households to include slaves. It may be that he's simply describing, as a matter of fact, what he sees going on around him; Athens had one of the largest slave populations in the ancient Greek world and most families would have had a slave. However, on the basis of what Aristotle has previously said, the only people who ought to be in that position are those individuals who are not equipped to manage their own affairs and accept that it is in their best interests for others to do so for them.

With regard to the place of women, it might be worth noting that for Aristotle 'by nature' simply means 'for the most part'; it refers to what usually happens. Based on his observations in the culture of his day, women tended to be under the control of men and, in so far as this is what generally happened, it was the natural state of affairs. For Aristotle, the reason for this is simple: in general, men tend to be physically stronger than women. This is just a biological observation. In one sense, then, women are literally the weaker sex. But Aristotle is quick to add that, because of this, women have been adapted by nature to have more acute senses than men – being physically weaker they need to be more aware of potential threats in the environment. This superior perception gives women an advantage when it comes to intellectual activity. Looking at differences between the sexes across multiple species, Aristotle is of the view that, in general, males are stronger and more aggressive, but also dim-witted, while females are gentler and more intelligent. Women, then, tend to be subordinate to men owing to their relative lack of physical strength, but in the attribute that Aristotle repeatedly says is the defining characteristic of human beings – intelligence – they are superior. Men may tend to dominate politically and take control of the affairs of the city, but this is in fact a hindrance to living what Aristotle thinks is the ideal life of quiet philosophical contemplation. Women are thus both physically and socially better placed to be philosophers than men, it seems. Aristotle clearly thinks that there are differences between men and women, a view based on his biological observations, but there is no suggestion that one sex is straightforwardly superior to the other. Both play their parts in the life of the community in different ways.

So, the city-state for Aristotle is the natural unit: it comes about organically and it enables its members to live a good life. It is the equivalent of the organism whose parts function for the sake of the whole. In this sense, the community comes first, and Aristotle says that it is 'prior to the individual'. And it is, literally: people are only ever born into communities – not just to two parents, but also within a wider group which can provide the protection, food, and other things that are necessary for the raising of children. Aristotle adds that people are almost always unable to sustain themselves when separated from their community. There may be the odd individual who might attempt to grow all their own food, make all their own clothes, and become completely self-reliant. But such a person will be cutting themselves off from their nature as a social animal and they are highly unlikely to have any free time left over to engage in reflective intellectual pursuits. For those two reasons, Aristotle would say that such a person is unable to live a fully human life. Focused entirely on subsistence, they'll be closer to an animal. A rich, human life requires more than that, and it's the city-state that provides the infrastructure to make it happen.

Aristotle goes on in the *Politics* to discuss what an ideal city-state might look like and what city-states actually look like in practice. As well as criticizing some of the proposals outlined by Plato in his *Republic* and *Laws*, Aristotle examines some of the constitutions of existing city-states, including Sparta, cities on Crete, and Carthage. His discussions are evidently based on information that he has gathered about these places. Like the good scientist he is, he's done his research; he's gathered together the information he needs in order to be able to make his observations. It is in this context that it is worth mentioning a remarkable discovery.

Around the end of the nineteenth century, a whole series of ancient texts were recovered from the sands of Egypt. Many of these came from the rubbish dumps of the ancient city of Oxyrhynchus, where a huge number of scraps of papyrus documents were found. Some of them related to everyday life, such as farming accounts and personal letters; some contained fragments of already well-known works, such as the epics of Homer. More exciting for many was the discovery of ancient texts that until this point had been completely lost. One such discovery was a work entitled *Constitution of the Athenians*. This particular papyrus – in fact, a set of four scrolls – didn't come from Oxyrhynchus but instead, most likely, from Hermopolis, a site a little further south along the Nile. The scrolls were bought in Cairo in 1890 for the British Museum and now reside in the British Library. A number of ancient sources credit this work to Aristotle and their quotations match what we find in the papyrus. It looked, then, as if a 'new' work by Aristotle had been found.

The *Constitution of the Athenians* was published for the first time in 1891 under Aristotle's name. Today many scholars doubt that Aristotle wrote it himself. Instead, it is thought to be the product of Aristotle's school, part of a larger-scale project to gather information about the constitutions of numerous city-states in the ancient world. It is the only survivor out of a collection said to have contained 158 constitutions. Perhaps it was written by a junior member of Aristotle's school, although, as we have noted, the ancient sources do not hesitate to credit it to Aristotle himself. It may have been listed as one of his works because he was the overall editor of the collection.

The work itself is a detailed report on the history of Athens' organization and how the city was then being run. This included recounting past conflicts between different groups within the city and recording the creation of laws that attempted to manage this. All the famous politicians in Athenian history, such as Solon and Pericles, are discussed, along with the changes they made to the running of the city. The political structures that were in place are also described: systems of voting, the role of magistrates, the function of the council, and so on. There's a sense in which Aristotle is describing the inner workings of an organism, just as he did when examining his fish on Lesbos. As then, what Aristotle is doing is gathering the hard empirical evidence necessary for any scientific study. In these ancient papyrus scrolls pulled from the sand, we can, then, witness the birth of the social sciences.

The historical tensions that Aristotle (or his junior research assistant) describes in Athenian politics open up a range of more theoretical questions about what the best organization of a city-state might be. For Aristotle, this ultimately comes down to managing the relationships between different classes in society. The goal is to find some kind of equilibrium that can work for everyone. Given what we've already seen, Aristotle thinks that everyone ought to play some part in the running of the city. That seems to rule out systems in which power is concentrated in one individual, such as monarchy. It's 'neither just nor expedient', he says, for one person to rule over everyone else. But what about different groups of people? In most real-world communities, there are divisions between groups often based on wealth. There's usually some concentration of wealth in the hands of a few, creating a poorer majority and a wealthy elite. The degree of concentration and inequality can vary quite a bit, but this basic pattern seems almost universal. Unsurprisingly, each of these two groups thinks that it should be in charge of the community. When the rich elite have control we have an oligarchy, and when the poorer masses are in charge we have democracy. Aristotle is against both these forms of government in their pure form because they prioritize the interests of one group over the well-being of the whole community. Instead, he suggests that some kind of mixed constitution is best, drawing on elements of both. The key is to avoid any polarized form of class conflict in which one section of society feels victimized by the other. The organism of the city-state needs to have all its parts working towards its common good, not fighting against each other.

This idea that we ought to avoid extremes and try to find a middle ground leads Aristotle to reflect on what he calls 'the people in the middle': the middle class. The problem with the wealthy is that they can often have a sense of entitlement and do not like being told what to do; they think the rules don't apply to them. The problem with the poor, as Aristotle saw it, is that they can become bitter and resentful; their lack of opportunity and control also means they fall into a habit of subservience. Neither of these is an ideal state to be in. As Aristotle puts it, 'the result is a State not of free men but of slaves and masters, the former full of envy, the latter of contempt'. A community like that is one that has gone wrong. What we want, Aristotle says, is instead one that is based on friendship and partnership, with members willing to share with each other. The people most likely to do this are those who are in broadly the same place in life, and these form the middle class. Ideally, the city-state should 'aim to consist as far as possible of those who are like and equal'. The way to do this is to expand the middle class as much as possible, lifting people out of poverty, curbing excessive wealth, and, in general, reducing inequality. These are of course all issues that are as relevant now as they were in fourth-century BC Athens. It is only by tackling these issues that we'll be able to have a strong, well-functioning political community. Aristotle was no great radical; we might describe him in today's terms as a centrist. But he would certainly be a critic of the extreme inequalities that are commonplace today – he would argue that such divisions will inevitably hinder the ability of our communities to function smoothly and to create the conditions required for everyone to enjoy a good life.

When Aristotle was still on Lesbos, he received an invitation from King Philip of Macedon to travel north and tutor the king's teenage son, Alexander (who would later become known as 'the Great'). Later sources suggest that this was due to Aristotle's immense reputation for wisdom, but it is far from clear that his reputation was really that established by this time; he was in his mid-forties and hadn't yet founded any school of his own. Another tradition suggests that Aristotle's father, Nicomachus, had been a doctor at the court of Philip's father, King Amyntas, so there may have been a personal connection. Philip was also on good terms with Hermias in Assos, so Hermias may have recommended him for the post. We don't know for sure. What we do know is that Aristotle accepted the invitation and headed north to Macedonia. Theophrastus went with him. We can only speculate, but one wonders if Aristotle saw this as an opportunity to share some of his thoughts about how a city-state could best flourish with someone being prepared for political leadership.

Aristotle taught his pupil for three years, until Alexander became regent when his father was away at war. Again, we don't know precisely what Aristotle taught him – generic school lessons, advice for princes, or a taste of the philosophical problems that Aristotle had learned at the Academy.

It seems that Alexander – perhaps the quintessential man of action – wasn't overly inspired by what he heard and was easily distracted by more active pursuits. There's no trace of any of Aristotle's ideas shaping Alexander's subsequent behaviour, and Aristotle makes no mention of Alexander in his works. Later writers make much of Alexander being Aristotle's most important pupil – he would certainly become the most famous – but there is no real evidence of any influence. Perhaps Alexander was a bored, impatient teenager with little interest in whatever his newest tutor was trying to teach him. In his *Nicomachean Ethics*, Aristotle commented that 'a young man is not a proper hearer of lectures on political science, for he is inexperienced in the actions that occur in life', and 'since he tends to follow his passions, his study will be vain and unprofitable'. Some have suggested that this may have been Aristotle reflecting on his own experience with the young Macedonian prince.

It seems that Aristotle stayed in Macedonia for a while even after his duties as tutor to Alexander had come to an end. He may have continued his biological research there, looking at species he'd not encountered at Lesbos. He finally left when Philip died a couple of years later, but we don't know why. Perhaps he'd benefited from an income granted by the king that came to an end with his death. Philip had in fact been murdered and this may have generated an atmosphere of political uncertainty. Or perhaps he had concerns about what Macedonia would be like under the leadership of his ex-pupil. Either way, it was at this point that Aristotle returned to Athens.

Alexander would soon head east, to war. He would

transform the ancient world in his wake. By the time the young king had finished, there were no independent Greek city-states left. The vast territory that he conquered, stretching all the way from Greece to India, was carved up after his death into three large kingdoms by his generals. In the short term, the previously independent cities around the Aegean came under the control of Macedonia. The political world that Aristotle had described and examined was suddenly no more.

This transformation of the Greek political landscape made Aristotle's careful study of the independent city-state almost immediately redundant. The world that he had been describing was now gone. Of course, there's no way he could have foreseen this. But he wasn't merely describing the political world as it existed in his day; he was also thinking about what type of community would be most conducive to people living a good life. As we have seen, his view is that people need to be actively involved in the running of their community, to feel invested in it, rather than merely passive subjects of a distant government. In the world that emerged in the decades after Alexander's conquests, that claim might have felt anything but redundant. As people had fewer opportunities to be involved in the running of their communities, they started to turn inwards and focus more on personal ethics than political theory. Although in one sense Aristotle's discussion of the self-governing city-state might have seemed no longer relevant, his analysis offered an explanation as to why people felt increasingly alienated and overlooked. While there are some elements in the *Politics* which people would rightly question today, that core idea remains as incisive now as it was when Aristotle first formulated it.

The Benefits of Literature

Athens was a pre-eminent centre of culture in the ancient world. It is no great surprise, then, that Aristotle decided to return there after Philip of Macedon's death. As we have just seen, one of the many reasons why Aristotle thought people should live in city-states is that they were large enough to sustain a rich cultural life, and nowhere did that better than Athens, with its vibrant community of philosophers, artists, and dramatists. Having lived there previously for twenty years, longer than he had lived anywhere else, it may simply have felt like home, even if he was officially an outsider. He may still have had friends at the Academy, and the Academy itself may have been a significant pull, as a community of like-minded people all pursuing philosophy. And as we know, Aristotle thought that enjoying a rich cultural life marked the difference between merely surviving and living a rich, interesting human life.

One of the high points of Athenian cultural life was its drama – both tragedy and comedy. Each year, at the festival of Dionysus, the Athenian population would come together to watch new plays performed and judged in competition. It was during Aristotle's second period in Athens that the Theatre of Dionysus, where the festival took place, was rebuilt on the southern slope of the Acropolis. This brand-new marble arena could hold some 15,000 people. Aristotle may well have been there to see its reopening. There, he would have also seen newly erected statues of Aeschylus, Sophocles, and Euripides, who had already become the three canonical tragedians, just as they are for us today. Although the earliest forms of tragedy may have started elsewhere, the art form was developed and perfected in Athens and these three iconic playwrights were all Athenians.

Aristotle was evidently a regular visitor to the theatre. In his book *Poetics*, he mentions many plays by a wide variety of writers, most of whose works are now sadly lost, as well as discussing those works of Aeschylus, Sophocles, and Euripides that have survived to the present day. Aristotle says that there are two things he is most interested in when it comes to drama and poetry – and we might extend this to include artworks in general – namely how they are made and the effect that they have on people. In order to know how to make them, we need to know what they are and what their component parts are. In this sense, his approach was ultimately no different from the one he took to studying animals and the rest of the natural world. He uses the same method no matter what his object of study is. What all the arts share, he says, is that they are types of imitation. In antiquity, philosophers such as Parmenides wrote in verse, but that didn't make their work poetry in the sense that Aristotle is concerned with in the *Poetics*, where his focus is on imitative artistic creation.

Imitation can take many forms; in drama, 'the poets imitate people doing things'. But why? Aristotle thinks there are a number of reasons for this. First, we enjoy seeing things represented in this way. This might be connected to the fact that as small children we learn through imitation, watching and copying the behaviour of others. It can help us to understand the world around us – in this case, the actions of others and the myriad varieties of social interaction. It is, then, a perfectly natural activity, Aristotle suggests, an expression of our nature as social animals trying to navigate human psychology.

Originally drama, and tragedy in particular, was very simple, with just one person presenting the story. Aristotle tells us that Aeschylus introduced a second actor, and then Sophocles added a third and started to use painting as scenery. These were not complex or expensive productions. Despite that simplicity, Aristotle identifies a number of component parts. The most important of these, he argues, is plot. Drama is not about people or characters as such; it is about actions and stories. Whether someone enjoys a good life or not depends on what they do and what happens to them, and drama is about exploring these things. The plots of tragedies tend to focus on sudden reversals of fortune, something that could befall any of us if we are unlucky. It's this recognition that gives drama the power to affect our emotions.

A successful piece of drama will present what Aristotle calls 'a complete action', from start to finish. A complete action will have a beginning, a middle, and an end. What he means by this is that the beginning ought to set things up without presupposing any specific events immediately before it. The end will bring things to a natural conclusion, resolving the story to the audience's satisfaction. The middle – the central action of the piece – will develop almost inevitably out of the opening scene-setting, but on its own will leave things unresolved, requiring the ending to complete the action. The whole thing should not go on too long and the audience should be able to hold all of the plot in their minds as it progresses. No doubt we've all seen excessively long and overly complex movies where it is difficult to keep up with what is happening. Aristotle had already warned against making those sorts of basic mistakes when constructing drama, over two thousand years before cinema was even invented.

A good plot also needs a sense of unity. Aristotle argues that there's little point in things happening to a character if they don't contribute in some way to the central story. Homer's *Odyssey*, for instance, doesn't tell us about everything that happened to Odysseus but only those things that are relevant to the story of his journey back home to Ithaca after the Trojan War. In drama, if a character is introduced early on and then disappears from view, we expect them to come back later in some meaningful way. If not, we might wonder why they were introduced at all. If something could be omitted without affecting the central story of the plot, then it is extraneous – not a part of the whole – and perhaps ought not to be included. Aristotle mentions examples from epic poetry as well as tragedy, and he thinks that his analysis of plot will apply to both. By extension, we can use it to think about movies and novels as well.

What about specifics? Aristotle talks about plot lines in which events come about 'contrary to expectation but because of one another'. The outcome is inevitable, but we didn't expect it. Such plots lines are good because they provoke emotional reactions from us. Chance events can also work well, but they do so best when it seems as if they might have happened for a purpose. We like it when a bad character is accidentally killed by some scheme of theirs that misfires – what we now often call 'poetic justice'. Aristotle himself gives a great example: 'the statue of Mitys in Argos killed the man who was responsible for Mitys' death by falling on top of him as he was looking at it'. It's a completely chance, random event, but it doesn't quite feel like it to us, the audience. Then there are sudden reversals of fortune – the king who becomes a beggar – or moments of recognition, when a stranger is suddenly identified as a long-lost relative. Although Greek tragedy usually focused on events befalling kings and their families, the stories nevertheless need to be relatable in order to affect us. We can only feel pity for the undeserved suffering of, say, Oedipus if we can identify with the character. It's the suffering of a fellow human being that we connect with, not the historical figure. That's one reason why tragic characters are often flawed. Like us, they are not perfect, and sometimes they make bad choices. The disaster that unfolds from just one poor decision is both something that we can relate to – for we all do the same from time to time – and a warning about the dangers that can follow. 'Look, this is what can happen if you do x, so take heed.'

Beyond plot, Aristotle also examines the importance of character and script. Characters need to be well formed and relatable; they need to act consistently and in ways appropriate to who they are. The words that are put into their mouths also matter, so the script needs to be well written. The good dramatist will need a thorough understanding of grammar,

Aristotle insists. Then there's the staging and production of drama, although Aristotle warns against giving this too much weight. It's the plot that is fundamental, and no amount of fancy staging can compensate for a weak story. One easy way to test this is to see what impact a play has from reading it compared to seeing it performed. A really strong piece of drama will work on the page, even if it was ultimately conceived as something to be seen by an audience.

Tragedy can be gruesome. Although the most graphic violence was not acted out on stage, the plot lines still had the power to shock. In Aeschylus' *Agamemnon*, Clytemnestra murders her husband Agamemnon in revenge for his sacrifice of their daughter. In the second instalment of the trilogy, the *Libation Bearers*, Clytemnestra is murdered in turn by her own son, Orestes, in revenge for the killing of his father. These sorts of stories can be gripping dramas, but they are not straightforwardly pleasurable. Aristotle notes various ways in which we might gain pleasure from the formal aspects of such plays: that the plot is well constructed and resolves itself in a satisfying conclusion, that the dialogue is well written, that it is performed well, and so on. But do we gain any pleasure from the tragic story itself? Aristotle thinks that we do. We can enjoy, he says, a pleasurable release when we experience extreme emotions such as pity and fear. He calls this a moment of 'purification' (*catharsis*), in which any excess of these emotions gets released, restoring us to a state of balance. Although he does not explicitly say this, we might also think that experiencing these extreme emotions in the safe space of the theatre can be useful training to help us cope with them later in real-life situations. One common theme in Greek tragedy is extreme grief or jealousy leading people to do terrible things. Seeing such extreme emotions on stage and sharing in them vicariously, not to mention seeing how badly things can go when they spiral out of control, might help us to manage those emotions better in our own lives.

Aristotle's ideas in the *Poetics* are invaluable for understanding Greek tragedy. He is an almost contemporary witness to one of the greatest periods of artistic production in history. But his ideas are far from being merely of antiquarian or academic interest, despite being over two thousand years old. His work is still being drawn on by people today. As one very successful guide to screenwriting reminds its readers, there's no secret, hidden wisdom about how to tell a story well; it's all been public knowledge for a very long time, because it is all there, set out in Aristotle's *Poetics*.

The *Poetics* as we have it today consists of one book devoted to the analysis of tragedy. At one point, Aristotle comments that he will discuss the other kind of drama, comedy, later, though he never does. This has led some to conclude that the text of the *Poetics* which has survived is incomplete and there must have been a second book devoted to comedy. One reason for thinking this is that, in his *Rhetoric*, Aristotle comments that he has already discussed in the *Poetics* the way that ludicrous things can be pleasant. Another is that an ancient list of Aristotle's works mentions a treatise on the art of poetry in two books. Much later, in the thirteenth century, when William of Moerbeke translated the *Poetics* into Latin, he ended his text with the comment that this was the *first* book of Aristotle's *De Arte Poetica*, suggesting that he was least at aware of the existence of a further book.

Alas, Book 2, if it existed, is now completely lost. As a consequence, frustratingly little information has come down to us about Aristotle's views on comedy, but he evidently thought that it was important. At the most important Athenian drama festival, playwrights would stage three tragedies and one comic satyr play. Perhaps some light relief at the end of proceedings, after all the murder and intrigue, was deemed prudent to lift everyone's spirits. Like tragedy and epic poetry, comedy was, Aristotle tells us, a form of imitation, a mirror reflecting back aspects of daily life. Unlike tragedy, comedy usually has a happy ending, he tells us, and 'no one gets killed by anybody'. It tends to portray inferior people, figures who are laughable, rather than the complex characters of serious drama. The incidents it portrays have to be believable so that we can identify with them. It too can generate a purification of emotions (*catharsis*) – laughter is the best medicine.

Those few comments can be found in the first book of the *Poetics*. The lost second book presumably focused on the details of comic plays, such as plot and stock characters, just as Aristotle had done for tragedy in Book 1. We find other comments on comedy in his *Nicomachean Ethics*, in a passage where he discusses the virtue of wit. Aristotle suggests that comedy, joking about, is an entirely appropriate thing to do when resting from the busyness of everyday life. Whether it be at a party or over dinner, it's good to be able to tell jokes and make light of things. Someone who doesn't do this, or doesn't know how to do this, Aristotle describes as a bore. However, someone who goes too far, continually playing the fool, he calls a buffoon. These are the two extremes, two vices, to be avoided and the virtue of wit falls in between. The sort of refined sense of humour that Aristotle seems to have in mind will avoid excessive crudity and offence. His preference seems to have been for the more polite comedy of manners which was developing in his day and would become known as 'New Comedy', often associated with Menander, who was himself a pupil at the Lyceum, rather than the often bawdy 'Old Comedy' of Aristophanes, full of swearing and obscene jokes.

One way in which our own use of comedy ought not to overstep its bounds, Aristotle suggests in the *Nicomachean Ethics*, is by avoiding being deliberately offensive. He also argues that comedy on stage ought to be fun, relaxing, and entertaining, and so shouldn't cause pain to anyone else. The goal is relaxation and amusement, not provocation. Bearing in mind Aristotle's stress on the importance of living within a harmonious community, humour too ought to contribute to this by generating enjoyable social occasions – moments to bring the community together – rather than upsetting or alienating anyone. This issue is as current today as it was when Aristotle reflected on it. Where do we draw the lines between humour and offence? Should some topics be off limits for comedy? Aristotle's concern was with what sort of person we want to be: do you want to be the sort of person who laughs at jokes that you know will deeply upset others? More to the point, if you know that a certain type of joke is likely to deeply offend some people, would you tell it anyway? The context of Aristotle's discussion of wit suggests that this isn't about, say, the provocative stand-up comic who is deliberately trying to push the boundaries, but instead what you or I might say at a social event where everyone just wants to unwind and relax. The person with the virtue of wit will have enough tact to avoid making jokes that might have the potential to cause offence.

Alongside tragedy and comedy, Aristotle also mentions music as an art that can give us a much-needed emotional release. For all three, we might think of current examples where Aristotle's basic idea rings true: the heartbreaking drama where we witness first hand the traumatic experiences of the main characters; the horror movie that puts us through extreme fear followed by a sense of relief at the end; the slapstick comedy where we laugh at the accidents and misfortunes of others; the bittersweet love song through which we relive the emotions of a failed relationship. In all these cases, a work of art can prompt us to experience difficult emotions in a relatively safe, artificial setting, helping us to process the real emotions that befall us in our own lives. If managing those emotions is essential for anyone wanting to live a good life – and tragedy shows us all too well what happens to characters who don't do this – then these art forms are absolutely essential. There's a reason why cinema, television, and music, not to mention theatre and literature, have become such major industries in the present day. At their best, they serve a vital purpose.

It might come as a surprise to some to see Aristotle – the hard-nosed scientist trying to uncover the secrets of nature – pay all this attention to works of fiction. One might expect him to have more time for, say, history than for tragedy or epic poetry. The historian, Aristotle says, is someone who 'says what has happened' whereas the poet merely says 'the kind of thing that would happen'. Surely the facts of history would appeal more to the mind of a scientist. Not so. Aristotle says in no uncertain terms that 'poetry is more philosophical and more serious than history'. Why is that? His answer is simple: history deals with particular truths – the Battle of Salamis took place in 480 BC, for instance – but poetry expresses universal truths about the human condition. Although the characters in ancient Greek tragedy and poetry were named after figures who existed (or were thought to have existed), it would be a mistake to think that we are seeing or reading stories about these particular individuals. What matters are the universal truths that we can extract from these tales – that one bad decision can lead to disastrous consequences, that violence begets violence, that emotions out of control can be dangerous. These are issues that any thoughtful human being ought to reflect on from time to time. Aristotle understood this.

As we have already seen, one of the reasons why Aristotle admired the city-state – the medium-sized political community – was that it was large enough to sustain a culture that could produce and stage this kind of drama, making this kind of reflection on the human condition available to all its citizens. For us, good movies and good novels can also do the same. Enjoying these things is not merely an idle distraction to occupy our spare time away from work; it's an essential part of living a rounded human life.

A Good Life

When it came to thinking about how people ought to live and what it means to enjoy a good human life, Aristotle brought to bear both sides of his intellectual background. On the one hand, he approached the topic as a biologist, drawing on his studies of animals. On the other, he drew on his experience as a student of Plato, when he had spent much time reflecting on the nature of goodness in a far more abstract manner.

Aristotle opens the lectures that we now know as the *Nicomachean Ethics* by asking what it is that people want from life. What is the highest good, the thing that we want most of all? What do we pursue for its own sake and what do we pursue for the sake of something else? Take the example of money. It's something that we all pursue to a greater or lesser extent, because we all need it in order to live. We want it because of what we can buy with it and what it can enable us to do. However, the money in itself isn't very interesting at all. We don't want it for its own sake, but for the sake of other things, whether that be food, clothes, or a nice holiday. As such, Aristotle calls it merely an 'instrumental good'. He contrasts this with what he calls 'intrinsic goods', those things that are worth having for their own sake. There are also some things we pursue that are both valuable in themselves and desired for the sake of something else. What Aristotle wants to isolate is the one thing – if it exists – that is only ever pursued for its own sake and never for the sake of anything else. Such a thing would be the highest good. It would be the ultimate goal of everything we do.

Is there such a thing? Aristotle thinks that there is: happiness. What we all want is to live a happy life. We might disagree about what a happy life might look like or what we need in order to achieve it, but ultimately we are all after the same thing. If someone were to ask us *why* we want to be happy, we would probably be a bit confused. Surely that is self-evident, for everyone wants to be happy. Not only that, but there is no explanation that we could possibly give, because, as the highest good, happiness is not for the sake of anything else. We want to be happy because we want to be happy, and that's that. It's the point where all justifications and explanations come to an end.

So, according to Aristotle, we all want happiness and this is the highest good. But how to attain it? The Greek word translated as 'happiness' here is *eudaimonia*, which is sometimes rendered as 'well-being', 'flourishing', or simply 'a good life'. It means something more than simply the subjective, potentially fleeting, feeling that is sometimes associated with the English word 'happiness'. What Aristotle has in mind is the idea that your life as a whole is objectively going well and that other people will be able to recognize this. This, he says, is what we all want – not some passing sensation of 'feeling happy'.

What is involved in our life flourishing in this way? This is where Aristotle brings his biologist's mindset into play. If we think about parts of the human body, a good eye is one that can see well and a good heart is one that pumps blood effectively. Each organ has its function, and a good example of an organ is one that fulfils its function well. Similarly, Aristotle suggests, a good human being will be one that fulfils its function well. As we saw earlier, Aristotle thinks that the function of complete organisms is to stay alive and to reproduce. That's a function which we share with other living beings. But is there a uniquely human function, something that humans are *for*, in the same way that the eye is *for* seeing? It can't be simply being alive, which we share with plants, nor being able to perceive and move, which we share with other animals. The distinctively human function is, as we've seen earlier, our ability to think rationally, or, as Aristotle puts it, 'activity of the soul in accordance with reason'. A good human being is one that thinks and acts rationally. When we do this, we are functioning as we should as rational animals, and 'happiness' or 'well-being' is the name for that proper functioning.

As we can see, happiness and function are two key notions in Aristotle's thinking about how to live a good life. A third, equally key, notion is virtue. As with 'happiness', it is important here to think about the issue of translation. The Greek word that Aristotle uses is *aretē*, which means something like 'excellence', and so its meaning is a little wider than just moral virtue. When we describe something as 'having many virtues', we mean that it has many strengths, not that it is morally good, and it's that sense of 'virtue' which is useful to keep in mind. If, in this sense, 'virtue' simply means 'something that is excellent', then we can immediately see the connection between this notion and the idea of something that is fulfilling its function well.

Aristotle talks about lots of different virtues that people can have, as well as the more general idea of someone being virtuous. One of the key points that he wants to get across is that when we act virtuously or excellently, we are fulfilling our function as both rational and social animals. When we do this, we experience pleasure – a welcome by-product – and we enjoy a good, happy life. There is no conflict, then, between acting well towards others and our own self-interest, because when we act sociably, we are being good social animals, which enables us to flourish as individuals. Indeed, if we were to act antisocially, we'd go against our nature as social animals, generating internal conflict that would stop us from achieving the one thing that we really want – happiness.

So, in order to live a good, happy life, we need to become virtuous, which means developing a range of positive character traits that befit a human being. Aristotle distinguishes between what he calls 'intellectual' and 'moral' virtues. Among the intellectual virtues, he includes the sorts of things that require our rationality: the ability to gain knowledge through the use of logical reasoning; to know how to make things; to know how to make good, rational decisions; to have philosophical understanding or wisdom; to be intelligent. Among the moral virtues, he includes a wide variety of traditional virtues, such as courage, moderation, generosity, and friendliness. He defines each of these moral virtues as intermediate points between the extremes of two associated vices. For instance, cowardice is clearly a vice – no one wants to be a coward. At the other extreme is recklessness, where someone has no regard for their safety at all. That's equally a vice, in the sense of being a character trait we'd prefer not to have. Standing in the middle ground between these two opposed extremes is the virtue of courage, which sometimes prompts us to take risks for the right reasons in certain circumstances, but not recklessly. Another interesting example which Aristotle discusses is connected to ambition. When taken to an extreme, ambition can certainly be a vice, Aristotle suggests, and its opposite, disengaged laziness uninterested in achieving anything, is equally something to be avoided. Between these two extremes, there will be a virtue, a sensible middle ground, although Aristotle doesn't know what to call it. But one thing is clear, the extremes are to be avoided. In his other set of lectures on ethics, known as the *Eudemian Ethics* (which are distinct from, but in part overlapping with, the *Nicomachean Ethics*), Aristotle lays out many of these sets of vices and virtues in a table, listing the two extreme vices, followed by the virtue that falls between them.

This idea that virtues fall in the middle between two extremes is sometimes referred to as 'the golden mean', the sensible middle ground. The moderate person avoids being both miserly and self-indulgent. Nothing to excess. That doesn't sound especially exciting. It's not a proposition that is likely to inspire the young. But it is something that rings true to anyone who has been around for a while. Excess can be good fun in short bursts, but it can't be sustained over any length of time. Someone with a fair amount of life experience will also know that it can be difficult to strike the right balance. Just where is the middle ground? It requires a good deal of experience and a certain amount of intuitive judgement. Aristotle describes it like this:

> It is a difficult business to be good, because in any given
> case it is difficult to find the mid-point (or mean) . . . it
> is easy to get angry – anyone can do that – or to give and
> spend money, but to feel or act towards the right person to
> the right extent at the right time for the right reason in the
> right way – that is not easy, and it is not everyone that can
> do that. Hence, to do these things well is a rare, laudable,
> and fine achievement.

Given the difficulty of the task, Aristotle goes on to say that
we ought to show understanding and be lenient to people who
sometimes go astray. After all, don't we all do so from time to
time? People who go severely astray should of course be held
accountable; but, again, deciding where to draw the line between minor and serious moral mistakes is not always clear-
cut, and ultimately it is a matter of judgement. As Aristotle
comments, 'it is not easy to define by a rule for how long, and
how much, someone may go wrong before they incur blame'.

This idea of a prudent middle path between two extremes
is not unique to Aristotle. We find it already in ancient Greek
culture, such as the Delphic maxim 'nothing in excess'; and,
at one point in the *Republic*, Plato had Socrates argue that
one ought to follow a middle path, avoiding the extremes on
either side, 'for this is the surest way to the highest human
happiness'. Aristotle was simply taking up an idea already in
circulation which struck him as important. We might also
note that this idea arose independently in other cultures too,
such as the Buddha's recommendation to follow a middle
way between the extremes of decadence and asceticism, and
Confucius' statement that 'the mean is supreme'. When the

greatest Greek, Indian, and Chinese philosophers all agree on a point, it is probably one worth considering very seriously.

So far we have seen Aristotle talk about intellectual virtues and moral virtues. Ideally, we ought to try to embody them all. But different ways of life may put more emphasis on some than on others. When thinking about what a good life for a human being might look like, Aristotle considers a number of competing options. What is it that we ought to pursue? He dismisses out of hand a life devoted to making money, the sort of thing that someone would do only if they had to; such a life is mistakenly devoted to something that is self-evidently only an instrumental good. He also considers a life devoted to the pursuit of pleasure. This is the life that most people lead, he says, because they mistakenly think that pleasure will bring them happiness. While it might be a reasonable thing to pursue from time to time, it would be a mistake to think that it is the highest good. A life focused just on the pursuit of pleasure might be suitable for animals, but it is not appropriate for a rational human being. With these out of the way, Aristotle thinks there are just two other, more serious contenders.

The first is what he calls a 'political' way of life, which he associates with the pursuit of honour or a good reputation. This is the life of the active, engaged citizen who plays a full part in their community and, as such, it expresses our nature as social animals. Such a person wants to act well within the community, be seen to act well, and be praised by their peers. They want to be admired and respected. In order to succeed in this way of life, they are going to need the moral virtues. They'll benefit from intellectual virtues too, especially the ability to make good decisions, but we might say that the moral virtues take centre stage.

The second is what we earlier called 'the contemplative life', a life devoted to trying to understand ourselves and the world around us, the life of the philosopher or scientist. This expresses our nature as rational animals. Both of these ways of life, highlighting different aspects of human nature, are appropriate and praiseworthy, Aristotle says. Even so, it seems fairly clear that Aristotle had a strong preference for the contemplative life as the highest ideal for a human, or at least for himself. While the life of the engaged citizen is clearly admirable, one of Aristotle's concerns is that it is in part dependent on the opinions of others. You can only be well thought of in your community if other people think it. The contemplative life, by contrast, is self-sufficient, not dependent on anyone else.

When we think about living a good life, we ought not to forget that this is *living* a good life – it's an activity, a process; it's the things that we do. It's not as if there's an ideal state of well-being that we can reach and, when we do, everything will be fine for ever. That's not how life works. Life is an ever-changing and ongoing process, a long, winding journey from birth to death. Once again, Aristotle's biological research may have informed his thinking here, but we should also recall his more abstract reflections about the nature of actuality and potentiality. A human being, he said, was a creature with a certain set of abilities or capacities. But a human who just lies still and does nothing is little different from a corpse. It's not enough merely to have these capacities, we have to make use of them – that's what being alive is all about. Rather than think about what we *are*, we ought instead to think in terms of what we *do*.

Similarly, Aristotle thought we ought to understand happiness as an activity. He argued that it would be rather odd to say that someone is happy when they are asleep. Happiness is not something that merely belongs to someone as a disposition; it is a characteristic of a life that is going well. As the highest good, it must relate to an activity that is intrinsically good, not done for the sake of anything else. Virtuous actions are intrinsically good – we do them because they are the right thing to do, not because of any benefit we might get from them. So, he concludes, it looks as if doing virtuous deeds – doing intrinsically good things – may be the key to happiness. Once again, it's not about 'being virtuous' in the sense of having some quality, it's about *acting* in a certain way, *doing* the right thing. If we describe someone as, say, generous, it should only be because they consistently act in generous ways.

This idea that we ought to understand human life as activity (and a good, happy human life as virtuous activity) led Aristotle to reject the notion we should value periods of doing nothing. For many people, after a hard week's work, it's the idle relaxation and amusement of the weekend that is the highlight they look forward to. But it would be a mistake, Aristotle suggests, to think that's where we'll find happiness. It would be strange if it turned out that all the troubles and hardships of life were simply for the sake of idle amusement. That can't be the goal. We all need rest and some downtime, of course, but those moments of relaxation are *for the sake of* activity, to enable us to recharge before returning to the business of life.

But what should the business of life be? What should we do? Unsurprisingly, people do a wide range of different things, and a flourishing and cultured human community presupposes a degree of specialization and division of labour. Aristotle would presumably say that, whatever we find ourselves doing, we ought to do it with the virtues in mind and as best we can. But of course he also wants to know what the highest or most important human activity might be. As we have already seen, Aristotle believes that the defining characteristic of human beings is our rationality – and so the intellectual virtues are in some ways the most important. The best activity that we can spend our time on is thinking, doing philosophy, and the highest form of life for a human being is a life devoted to intellectual inquiry and contemplation.

Not everyone of course can devote their entire lives to contemplation. Indeed, perhaps no one can, for to do so would be to live an almost disembodied life of thought, out of step with the realities of being human. It would be like trying to live the life of a god, Aristotle comments. But he is nevertheless quite insistent that it's the activity of philosophical reflection which is the most enjoyable of virtuous activities. It's also one of the most self-sufficient things that we can do, in the sense that we don't need any expensive equipment or materials simply to take some time out to pause and think, to consider deeply the sorts of big questions with which we've seen Aristotle himself grapple. All we really need is some time. A moment ago, we saw Aristotle dismiss the idea that idle relaxation is central to a good life, even if we all need a break every so often. Despite that, he does stress the importance of what he calls 'leisure time'. If we are to be able to engage in what Aristotle thinks is the defining human activity – rational reflection about the world and our place within it – then we need time free from practical demands in order to do so. We need time off from mundane work and responsibilities, but this will not be inactive, idle amusement; this will be the most important form of activity there is – the activity of the mind. Not all of us will be able to devote our entire lives to this kind of life of the mind, but perhaps we can try to build moments of reflection into our regular routines. Aristotle is quite insistent that, if we fail to do so, there will be a sense in which we are not living fully human lives. But equally, if that's all we do, perhaps we'll also be failing by going too far. Once again, the right path probably lies somewhere in the middle.

A Life of Inquiry

Aristotle spent the final period of his life in Athens. When he returned after his time in Macedonia, the Academy had a new head, Xenocrates, who had taken over after the death of Plato's nephew Speusippus in 339 BC. This was perhaps the second time that Aristotle was passed over for someone else. Although Xenocrates was slightly older than Aristotle, they would have been students together under Plato, and Aristotle may have felt it odd to return to the Academy under the leadership of someone he might have considered a contemporary and equal. Alternatively, he may have had little intellectual respect for Xenocrates, who was described by one ancient source as slow and sluggish. Comparing the two, Plato is reported to have said that, while Xenocrates needed a spur, Aristotle needed a bridle. One can imagine that the intellectual colt had no desire to be led by a lumbering packhorse. Beyond any personal differences, Aristotle's intellectual interests were now quite different from the abstract metaphysics that he had studied at the Academy in his youth. Since then, he had spent considerable time trying to understand the natural world, gathering material for his studies of animals. His close friend and collaborator Theophrastus was also doing the same for his own studies of plants. It was time for Aristotle and Theophrastus to set up their own school.

There were three gymnasia or public parks close to the city of Athens. The Academy was one, a short distance northwest of the centre. Another was the Cynosarges, to the south. The third was the Lyceum, east of the city, and this is where Aristotle and Theophrastus decided to base themselves. Their choice was not without precedent, for Socrates used to go there sometimes to discuss philosophy. There has been much debate about what sort of institutions the Academy and the Lyceum were. Both are named after public places of exercise, but now these names are primarily associated with the centres of learning established by Plato and Aristotle. It seems probable that, in both cases, like-minded people would gather to discuss philosophical questions in these public parks and, over time, property was bought nearby which could form a sort of private base of operations. We know that Plato owned a private garden close to the public Academy. The same seems to be the case with the Lyceum. As an outsider, Aristotle would not have been allowed to own property, but in the first instance he may have simply rented somewhere. Eventually property was acquired and owned by Theophrastus, but possibly not until after Aristotle's death.

The private property that formed the base of operations for the Aristotelian Lyceum included a garden, a number of houses, and a *peripatos*, which might refer to a colonnade or perhaps a tree-lined avenue (the word refers to a place to walk). It was from this last element that members of Aristotle's school gained the name 'Peripatetics', the 'people who gathered at the *peripatos*'. It has sometimes been thought that this word referred to Aristotle's habit of walking when teaching, but that is now largely rejected. The image of philosophers walking around while in deep discussion probably fitted the Academy better than the Lyceum. In Aristotle's works, based on his lectures, we often find references to diagrams, tables, and other visual aids, which make it natural to assume that he taught from a fixed location using the ancient equivalent of a blackboard. There would also have been a collection of books – the core of which would presumably have been Aristotle's own library amassed through his book collecting – and, at one point, Theophrastus refers to the setting up of maps on walls as aids to research. Among other materials that were gathered for study, Aristotle bought the books that had previously belonged to Speusippus. He is said to have paid an enormous sum for these and it is tempting to speculate that perhaps they included books once owned by Plato which Speusippus had inherited. Perhaps no one at the Academy thought they were worth acquiring, but Aristotle knew the value of a well-stocked research library.

What kind of institution was the Lyceum? Indeed, is 'institution' too grand a name to describe whatever it was? It has often been characterized as an educational institution, an ancient proto-university, with the implication that it had a body of students who were there to be taught. It is far from clear, though, that this was its primary mission. There is no reason to believe that Aristotle was motivated to become a teacher or that he would have taken payment for teaching. As we have seen, he was first and foremost a researcher, a scientist, someone devoted to trying to understand the world in which he lived. The Lyceum at its core was a small group of like-minded individuals who shared that passion for knowledge. If Aristotle gave lectures on different topics, it would likely have been to a small audience of peers – akin to a modern-day research seminar – rather than a larger audience of youths – like an undergraduate lecture. This was a private, inward-looking group of scholars, not an outward-facing school, although it was probably not a completely closed group, and no doubt welcomed interested new members as they came along.

Our words 'scholar' and 'school' come from the same Greek word, scholē, which referred to leisure or free time. A scholar is someone who has the leisure time to pursue their intellectual interests. Indeed, in his Nicomachean Ethics, Aristotle noted that leisure was one of the things required for anyone to do philosophy. You don't need much else, but you do need time. You also need not to be overburdened with distracting practical responsibilities, and to have the basic necessities of life covered. In short, you need not to have to work too much, and ideally not at all. The Lyceum was a community of scholars in this sense, individuals wealthy enough not to have to work all day, giving them the free time to be able to devote themselves to intellectual pursuits such as philosophy and science. If one kept one's day-to-day needs in check, this needn't require a fortune, but it did require some independent means.

In 323 BC, Alexander the Great died, far away in Babylon. Although this made no direct impact on the politics of Athens, which, as we've seen, was under the control of the Macedonians, the death of the ultimate source of Macedonian power led many in Athens – the once-proud democracy – to start to express more openly their hostility towards their foreign rulers. Aristotle was unsurprisingly caught in the middle of all this: he had worked for Philip of Macedon and tutored Alexander. The Lyceum was probably funded by money that he had earned when employed by Philip and it may have been perceived as ultimately a Macedonian organization. Aristotle felt under threat and decided that it would be prudent to leave. He headed to Chalcis, about fifty miles north of Athens and once the home of his mother, where he may have already owned a property inherited from her side of the family. It is said that Aristotle claimed he was leaving Athens so that the Athenians could not sin against philosophy for a second time: in an ominous echo of the events that had led up to the trial and execution of Socrates, legal charges had been brought against Aristotle and, however baseless they may have been, he evidently felt in danger. It is difficult to know how real the threat was. There may have been an element of paranoia, or perhaps just enough uneasiness to make concentration on his intellectual pursuits impossible. At Chalcis, Aristotle may have set up a new school, for one ancient source suggests that he taught there. While he was absent from Athens, it seems likely that Theophrastus took control of the affairs of the Lyceum. However, these arrangements did not last long: within the year, Aristotle was dead, an exile from his friends and his adopted home. It feels like a somewhat dispiriting end to what had been an extremely rich life.

After Aristotle's death, Theophrastus became head of the Lyceum, if he wasn't already. Following some turbulence, the Macedonians reasserted political control over Athens, placing Demetrius of Phalerum in charge of the city. As it happened, Demetrius was a follower of Aristotle. Although their teacher had fled for his life, Theophrastus now had a friend in the highest place and Demetrius aided him in securing the Lyceum's property as a permanent base. Theophrastus remained head of the Lyceum for thirty-six years, until 287 BC. He was succeeded by Strato of Lampsacus, who was in turn succeeded by others. None of these later figures attained the intellectual heights of either Aristotle or Theophrastus and none of their works have survived. Despite its early glory years, the Lyceum didn't become a major intellectual centre, and it fairly quickly fell into decline.

Although the Lyceum did not leave a lasting mark on Athenian intellectual life, its real legacy can be found elsewhere, further south. In the wake of Alexander's death, the vast territory that he had conquered was divided up between a number of his generals. One of these, Ptolemy, took charge of Egypt, making the city of Alexandria his new home. At some time around 300 BC, Ptolemy decided to found a museum and library as a new centre of intellectual activity. He invited Theophrastus to come to Alexandria to help in creating this, but without success. He was more successful with Demetrius of Phalerum, who agreed to act as an adviser and ultimately became the first head of what would become the famous library of Alexandria. Strato of Lampsacus also spent time there, acting as tutor to the king's son, who would go on to become Ptolemy II. Demetrius continued in his role as head of the library under Ptolemy II. While there, he is said to have supervised the production of the Greek version of the Hebrew scriptures known as the Septuagint.

The library would develop into the largest and most important in the ancient world. It became a hub for a wide range of intellectual activity, from astronomy and mathematics to literary criticism. Many of the early figures associated with it were true polymaths, as Aristotle had been. Eratosthenes, who became head of the library under Ptolemy III, engaged in literary criticism, history, mathematics, poetry, and geography. He is remembered today for calculating the circumference of the earth with incredible accuracy. Then there was Aristarchus, a pupil of Strato, who outlined a heliocentric model of the universe in the third century BC. In a different arena, Herophilus went beyond Aristotle's dissection of animals to start human dissection, which enabled him to discover the existence of nerves. Others did philological work on the text of Homer and the works of the great Athenian tragedians. If anywhere embodied Aristotle's multidisciplinary spirit of intellectual inquiry it was Alexandria, and this becomes much less surprising when we know that leading members of the Lyceum were instrumental in its creation.

In the first century BC, the texts we now know as Aristotle's came back into circulation after years of neglect. As we saw earlier, Aristotle's lecture notes had passed to Theophrastus, who in turn left them to his pupil, Neleus, and Neleus' relatives left them to moulder. When they were rediscovered, copied, and circulated, they quickly attracted attention and would go on to become a standard part of the philosophy curriculum in late antiquity, especially in Alexandria. The lectures of a number of late ancient philosophers were written up as commentaries on Aristotle's works. We have already noted the efforts of Boethius to translate Aristotle into Latin in the sixth century AD, who managed only the logical works. The same works were also translated into Syriac and, via these versions, into Arabic. Eventually almost all of Aristotle's works were translated into Arabic, and by the tenth century the great medieval city of Baghdad had become a flourishing centre of Aristotelian philosophy. In the twelfth century, Greek scholars in Constantinople assembled by the Byzantine princess Anna Comnena studied Aristotle's texts and wrote commentaries on works where they couldn't find an ancient one. A few decades later, in Muslim Spain, the great philosopher and jurist Ibn Rushd – known in the Latin west as Averroes – embarked on an ambitious plan to write multiple commentaries on each of Aristotle's works. Averroes would be an important influence on his contemporary, the renowned Jewish philosopher Maimonides. Attracted by the vibrant intellectual climate of Al-Andalus, scholars from various parts of Europe made the journey to Spain in search of scientific and philosophical knowledge. Among these was Gerard of Cremona, who travelled to Toledo, where he learned Arabic in order to translate Aristotle's *Physics* and a number of other works into Latin. A little later, the philosopher-scientist Michael Scot also translated works of Aristotle from Arabic to Latin, as well as translating a good number of Averroes' commentaries. In parallel with this Arabic–Latin translation movement, Aristotle's works were also translated directly from Greek into Latin. A key figure in this process was William of Moerbeke, active in the thirteenth century, but there had been others before him, such as James of Venice. One of Aristotle's most famous works, the *Nicomachean Ethics*, was translated by Robert Grosseteste, Bishop of Lincoln and the first chancellor of the University of Oxford.

By the mid-thirteenth century, almost all of Aristotle's works were available in Latin translation, and they inspired a burst of philosophical activity in the newly founded universities in Paris and Oxford. They were, however, far from uncontroversial. Within a few decades, the authorities at the University of Paris issued a condemnation of a range of Aristotelian ideas that conflicted with Christian teaching. Others took a more conciliatory path and attempted to marry Aristotelian philosophy with Christian theology. The most famous of these was Thomas Aquinas. Despite the condemnations, Aristotle quickly became central to the university curriculum from the thirteenth century right through to the early modern period. People referred to him simply as 'the Philosopher'. To study philosophy was to study Aristotle.

During the Italian Renaissance, there was a deliberate attempt by the new humanists to reject much of the culture of the Middle Ages and to reconnect directly with antiquity. For some, such as Francesco Petrarch, this meant a rejection of Aristotle, or at least a rejection of what he saw as his idolization by medieval scholastic philosophers. Others took a different view, challenging the medieval version of Aristotle by going back to ancient sources. In the case of Leonardo Bruni, this meant translating Aristotle afresh into humanistic Latin and stressing the humanist aspects of his thought, shifting the focus of attention from his works on logic and metaphysics to those dealing with politics, rhetoric, and poetics. As knowledge of Greek spread, the Renaissance goal of returning to the ideals of antiquity became in this context the study of Aristotle in Greek, free from medieval translations and commentaries, along with a fresh appraisal of his ancient Greek commentators. The great scholar-printer Aldus Manutius, based in Venice, made a vital contribution to this by printing all of Aristotle's works in Greek for the first time, at the very end of the fifteenth century.

There is an old story which claims that the development of modern science in the sixteenth and seventeenth centuries involved – indeed, required – a complete break with the existing Aristotelian tradition. He had become such an overwhelming figure of intellectual authority that his shadow was stifling progress. As Francis Bacon put it, 'knowledge derived from Aristotle, and exempted from the liberty of examination, will not rise again higher than the knowledge of Aristotle'. In truth, the situation was more complex than this narrative of wholesale rejection implies. A number of thinkers in the sixteenth century were all too aware from their close study of Aristotle's texts that he was a champion of observation and open inquiry. The problem was not with Aristotle himself, but with the way in which some people had come to read him. Jacopo Zabarella drew a distinction between the interpreter of Aristotle who is focused narrowly on what Aristotle wrote and the true Aristotelian who embraced his spirit of inquiry. It was a distinction between a focus on doctrine or on method, on the letter or the spirit of Aristotle's works. Around the same time, Alessandro Piccolomini commented that, in order to be a faithful Aristotelian, he would rely first and foremost on experience and observation, even if that meant disagreeing with Aristotle from time to time. In order 'to better imitate Aristotle', he wrote, 'I will leave Aristotle . . . each time the sense shows me the opposite to be true'. This, he added, is 'the authentic Aristotelian way of philosophizing', which 'in the name of reason and sense' will set aside the authority of all masters.

A particularly interesting example of this way of thinking can be found in Galileo Galilei. In Galileo's famous *Dialogue Concerning Two Chief World Systems*, he mocked the Aristotelians of his day for their slavish devotion to the letter of Aristotle's works regardless of what new evidence might be presented to them. Yet, along the way, Galileo commented that 'if Aristotle were now alive, he would change his opinion'. Galileo was happy to describe himself as an Aristotelian in Piccolomini's sense, free to depart from Aristotle's views when the evidence demanded. He could see that the sixteenth and seventeenth centuries' focus on observation and experimentation was in many ways thoroughly Aristotelian in spirit. Aristotle himself would have hated the idea that his works had become authoritative sources of rigid doctrine.

By the eighteenth century, Aristotle was largely seen as a relic of the past, still taught in a few backward-looking universities but for the most part dismissed as irrelevant to the exciting new developments of the Enlightenment. Classical scholars returned to him in the nineteenth century, primarily out of antiquarian interest. As his works were edited and translated afresh, in a context where he was no longer an overbearing authority figure, it became easier to assess him on his own terms. When Charles Darwin was given a recent translation of *Parts of Animals*, he was deeply impressed by the sophistication of Aristotle's biological observations. In the early twentieth century, the German classical scholar Werner Jaeger challenged the idea that Aristotle's works added up to a single, comprehensive, dogmatic body of doctrine – as they had often been seen previously – by arguing that they each came from a different stage in Aristotle's intellectual development. Aristotle once again became a fallible human being, whose early works reflected the strong influence of Plato but who later on broke free and asserted his intellectual independence. Authoritative works such as the *Metaphysics* were reassessed as slightly messy compilations of lecture notes written at different stages in Aristotle's life and gathered together by a later editor. This reassessment was also thoroughly Aristotelian in approach, for Aristotle himself did not shy away from critically examining the ideas and writings of his predecessors.

In the light of all this, it looks as if we can draw a clear distinction between two different ways in which we can use the word 'Aristotelian'. The first sense includes what we might call 'dogmatic Aristotelianism'. This often assumes that Aristotle left behind a single, systematic body of thought and that to be an Aristotelian means to subscribe to the truthfulness of this system, slavishly following the letter of his texts. There have certainly been plenty of dogmatic Aristotelians through the ages.

Aristotle himself, though, certainly wasn't dogmatic. His works do not add up to a single, unified system and he often discusses topics more than once in different places, offering potentially conflicting answers. Perhaps these, as has been suggested, reflect different stages in his intellectual development. Or perhaps they show him tackling the same problem from different directions, each one a fresh attempt to get closer to the truth. His writing is often tentative, putting forward plausible answers to complex questions, but always open to revision. Indeed, one of his translators has commented in frustration at his 'excessive tentativeness or caution', noting how often Aristotle uses the word 'perhaps'. In his works on animals, he is quite explicit about this: every theory is open to refutation by further observation. Nor was he enamoured of the idea of intellectual authority figures, famously commenting that, although he was a friend of Plato, he was a greater friend of the truth. He put forward ideas that he thought were true – or at least the most plausible – based on observation and argument, but it is difficult to imagine that he would have expected anyone to believe anything he said simply because he had said it.

Aristotle was committed to a life of inquiry, a life of continual investigation and observation in the pursuit of knowledge. It is this idea of open-minded and endlessly curious inquiry that can give us a second, and much better, sense of what it means to be an Aristotelian – the one that Zabarella, Piccolomini, and Galileo embraced. All human beings by nature desire to know. To be an Aristotelian in this second sense is simply to be a human being in the fullest possible way. It doesn't require us to accept anything that Aristotle said as true – indeed we might think that some of what he thought is now obviously false; instead, it simply involves joining him in the ongoing process of trying to understand the world in which we live. For naturally curious animals like us, it's what living the life of a human being is all about.

Guide to Aristotle's Texts

All Aristotle's surviving works are gathered together in *Aristoteles Graece*, edited by Immanuel Bekker and published in two volumes in Berlin in 1831 (the first two volumes of the five-volume *Aristotelis Opera*, 1831–70). Although there are more recent editions of many individual works, Bekker's edition remains a standard point of reference in so far as it is common practice to use his page, column, and line numbers to refer to specific passages in Aristotle's works. Bekker's edition, spread over two volumes, has continuous pagination. Each page is printed in two columns, standardly referred to by the letters 'a' and 'b'. Line numbers (5, 10, 15, 20, etc.) are printed down the middle of each page between the two columns. A typical 'Bekker reference' looks like this: 1245b12–14, referring to page 1245, column b, lines 12–14. That number on its own will guide you to the appropriate passage, even without the title of the individual work. These references are often printed in the margins of modern translations.

A second way to refer to Aristotle's works is to use the books and chapters (or just chapter for works in one book). For example, '*Nicomachean Ethics* 1.4' refers to Chapter 4 of Book 1 of that work. Books are usually referred to by numbers, but with Aristotle's *Metaphysics* the books are sometimes referred to by letters of the Greek alphabet, thus A.1, Γ.4, Θ.2, and so on. Someone who knows the basics of the Greek alphabet – alpha (A), beta (B), gamma (Γ) – might naturally assume that Book B is Book 2. However, matters are complicated by the fact that Book A is followed by Book α (often referred to as 'little alpha'), so in fact Book B is Book 3, and so on.

It is standard practice to refer to Aristotle's works by their traditional Latin titles, even though the texts themselves are in Greek. These Latin titles are often abbreviated. Thus, the *Nicomachean Ethics* is often referred to as *Ethica Nicomachea* or, more often, *Eth. Nic.*, or just *EN*, although sometimes *NE* is used, abbreviating the English title. This means that the same passage could be referred to in any of the following ways (or combinations thereof): *Nicomachean Ethics* 1.4 or *Eth. Nic.* 1.4, 1245b12–14 or just *EN* (or *NE*) 1245b12–14. But the Bekker reference alone, 1245b12–14, will always unambiguously guide you to the relevant passage of text.

On the opposite page I give a complete list of Aristotle's works, along with commonly used abbreviations, and Bekker's pagination. Bekker's edition includes a number of works no longer thought to be by Aristotle; I have not listed them here and their absence explains why the Bekker pagination is not continuous.

Beyond Bekker, fragments from Aristotle's lost works were gathered together by Valentin Rose in the fifth volume of *Aristotelis Opera* (1870); a revised edition published by Rose in 1886 has become the standard collection. In the late nineteenth century, a work entitled *Constitution of the Athenians* (*Ath. Pol.*) was discovered on papyrus and attributed to

ENGLISH TITLE	LATIN ABBREVIATION	BEKKER PAGES
Categories	Cat.	1–15
On Interpretation	Int.	16–24
Prior Analytics	An. Pr.	24–70
Posterior Analytics	An. Post.	71–100
Topics	Top.	100–164
Sophistical Refutations	Soph. El.	164–184
Physics	Phys.	184–267
On the Heavens	Cael.	268–313
On Generation and Corruption	Gen. Corr. (GC)	314–338
Meteorology	Meteor.	338–390
On the Soul	De An. (DA)	402–435
Shorter Natural Works	Parv. Nat.	436–480
History of Animals	Hist. An. (HA)	486–638
Parts of Animals	Part. An. (PA)	639–697
Movement of Animals	Mot. An. (MA)	698–704
Progression of Animals	Inc. An. (IA)	704–714
Generation of Animals	Gen. An. (GA)	715–789
Metaphysics	Metaph.	980–1093
Nicomachean Ethics	Eth. Nic. (EN)	1094–1181
Eudemian Ethics	Eth. Eud. (EE)	1214–1249
Politics	Pol.	1252–1342
Rhetoric	Rhet.	1354–1420
Poetics	Poet.	1447–1462

Aristotle when it was first published in 1891. It is now often thought to be a product of his school rather than by Aristotle himself, but it is regularly included in collected editions and translations of his works.

For many of Aristotle's individual works, the standard modern editions are now those in the Oxford Classical Texts series published by Oxford University Press. The Loeb Classical Library series, published by Harvard University Press, includes all Aristotle's works in Greek along with facing English translations.

The bulk of Aristotle's works were translated into English in twelve volumes as *The Works of Aristotle Translated into English*, edited by W. D. Ross, in 1908–52. This is often referred to as 'the Oxford translation'. It was revised and edited by Jonathan Barnes, and published in two volumes by Princeton University Press as *The Complete Works of Aristotle* in 1984. Known as 'the revised Oxford translation', it includes both the genuine and spurious works included in Bekker, along with a healthy selection of the fragments. It's the standard complete works of Aristotle in English.

There are numerous translations of individual works, especially those considered the most important. The Penguin Classics series includes translations of the *De Anima*, *Metaphysics*, *Nicomachean Ethics*, *Poetics*, *Politics*, and *Rhetoric*. I have quoted from a number of different translations in this book – Penguin, Oxford, Loeb – and in some cases have provided my own.

Further Reading

For readers who would like to delve further into Aristotle, the following introductions offer fuller overviews of his philosophy: G. E. R. Lloyd, *Aristotle: The Growth and Structure of his Thought* (Cambridge: Cambridge University Press, 1968); J. L. Ackrill, *Aristotle the Philosopher* (Oxford: Clarendon Press, 1981); Jonathan Lear, *Aristotle: The Desire to Understand* (Cambridge: Cambridge University Press, 1988); Jonathan Barnes, *Aristotle: A Very Short Introduction* (Oxford: Oxford University Press, 2000); Christopher Shields, *Aristotle* (London: Routledge, 2007).

BIOGRAPHY

There is an ancient biography of Aristotle in Diogenes Laertius' *Lives of the Eminent Philosophers* (5.1–35). A number of other ancient biographies also survive and these can be found in Ingemar Düring's *Aristotle in the Ancient Biographical Tradition* (Göteborg: Elanders, 1957). The groundbreaking modern biography of Aristotle is Werner Jaeger's *Aristotle: Fundamentals of the History of His Development* (1934; 2nd edn, Oxford: Clarendon Press, 1948; orig. German 1923). The best recent life is Carlo Natali's *Aristotle: His Life and School* (Princeton: Princeton University Press, 2013; orig. Italian, 1991).

CHAPTER 1: THE CONTEMPLATIVE LIFE

For further information about Plato's Academy and the archaeological site, see Paul Kalligas *et al.* (eds), *Plato's Academy: Its Workings and Its History* (Cambridge: Cambridge University Press, 2020). The fragments of Parmenides' poem can be found translated in many places, including Jonathan Barnes's *Early Greek Philosophy* (Harmondsworth: Penguin, 1987). For Aristotle's fragmentary *On Ideas*, see Gail Fine's *On Ideas: Aristotle's Criticism of Plato's Theory of Forms* (Oxford: Clarendon Press, 1993). For his response to Parmenides, see Timothy Clarke, *Aristotle and the Eleatic One* (Oxford: Oxford University Press, 2019). On Aristotle's metaphysics, and especially the idea that being is connected with activity, see Aryeh Kosman's *The Activity of Being: An Essay on Aristotle's Ontology* (Cambridge, MA: Harvard University Press, 2013).

CHAPTER 2: STUDYING NATURE

On Aristotle's researches on Lesbos, see Armand Marie Leroi's *The Lagoon: How Aristotle Invented Science* (London: Bloomsbury, 2014), written by a practising biologist. For an up-to-date collection of studies on Aristotle's biological works, see Sophia M. Connell (ed.), *The Cambridge Companion to Aristotle's Biology* (Cambridge: Cambridge University Press, 2021). The modern revival of interest in Aristotle's biological works was in part prompted by the publication of Allan Gotthelf and James G. Lennox (eds), *Philosophical Issues in Aristotle's Biology* (Cambridge: Cambridge University Press, 1987). Theophrastus' works on botany are *History of* [or *Enquiry into*] *Plants* and *Causes* [or *Explanations*] *of Plants*, both available in the Loeb Classical Library published by Harvard University Press.

CHAPTER 3: A RATIONAL ANIMAL

A classic modern account of Aristotle's logic can be found in Jan Łukasiewicz, *Aristotle's Syllogistic from the Standpoint of Modern Formal Logic* (Oxford: Clarendon Press, 1951). On the influence of the *Categories* in the Middle Ages, see Lloyd A. Newton (ed.), *Medieval Commentaries on Aristotle's Categories* (Leiden: Brill, 2008). On the problem of the sea battle, see Christopher Shields, *Aristotle* (London: Routledge, 2007), pp. 181–91, and Richard Sorabji, *The Philosophy of the Commentators, 200–600 AD: A Sourcebook, Volume 2: Physics* (London: Duckworth, 2004), pp. 111–16.

CHAPTER 4: SOCIAL ANIMALS

On Aristotle's political philosophy, see the essays in Marguerite Deslauriers and Pierre Destrée (eds), *The Cambridge Companion to Aristotle's Politics* (Cambridge: Cambridge University Press, 2013); and on the issue of slavery, Pierre Pellegrin's essay 'Natural Slavery', in that volume, pp. 92–116. On women in Aristotle's thought, see Sophia M. Connell, *Aristotle on Women: Physiology, Psychology, and Politics* (Cambridge: Cambridge University Press, 2021). For Aristotle's role as Alexander the Great's tutor, discussed within the wider context of Alexander's life, see Robin Lane Fox, *Alexander the Great* (London: Allen Lane, 1973).

CHAPTER 5: THE BENEFITS OF LITERATURE

For an introduction to Aristotle's *Poetics*, see Stephen Halliwell, *Aristotle's Poetics* (London: Duckworth, 1986). On Aristotle's lost second book of the *Poetics*, see Richard Janko, *Aristotle on Comedy: Towards a Reconstruction of Poetics II* (London: Duckworth, 1984), especially pp. 63–9. On further ways in which Aristotle might be relevant to the study of literature, see Robert Eaglestone, *Truth and Wonder: A Literary Introduction to Plato and Aristotle* (Abingdon: Routledge, 2022).

CHAPTER 6: A GOOD LIFE

For good introductions to Aristotle's ethics, see J. O. Urmson, *Aristotle's Ethics* (Oxford: Blackwell, 1988); David Bostock, *Aristotle's Ethics* (Oxford: Oxford University Press, 2000); and Michael Pakaluk, *Aristotle's Nicomachean Ethics: An Introduction* (Cambridge: Cambridge University Press, 2005). A number of classic papers on specific issues are reprinted in Amélie Oksenberg Rorty (ed.), *Essays on Aristotle's Ethics* (Berkeley, CA: University of California Press, 1980).

CHAPTER 7: A LIFE OF INQUIRY

On the history and organization of Aristotle's Lyceum, see John Patric Lynch's *Aristotle's School: A Study of a Greek Educational Institution* (Berkeley, CA: University of California Press, 1972), and Carlo Natali's *Aristotle: His Life and School* (Princeton: Princeton University Press, 2013; orig. Italian, 1991), chapters 2–3. The ancient evidence for Theophrastus' life and works is gathered together in William W. Fortenbaugh *et al.* (eds), *Theophrastus of Eresus: Sources for His Life, Writings, Thought and Influence*, 2 vols (Leiden: Brill, 1992). Similar collections for later members of the Lyceum can be found in Fritz Wehrli, *Die Schule des Aristoteles*, 10 vols (Basel: Schwabe, 1944–59). The ancient commentary tradition is examined in Richard Sorabji (ed.), *Aristotle Transformed: The Ancient Commentators and Their Influence*, 2nd edn (London: Bloomsbury, 2016). For Aristotle's subsequent influence, see, for instance, F. E. Peters, *Aristotle and the Arabs: The Aristotelian Tradition in Islam* (New York: New York University Press, 1968); Fernand Van Steenberghen, *Aristotle in the West: The Origins of Latin Aristotelianism* (Louvain: Nauwelaerts, 1955); Charles B. Schmitt, *Aristotle and the Renaissance* (Cambridge, MA: Harvard University Press, 1983); Craig Martin, *Subverting Aristotle: Religion, History, and Philosophy in Early Modern Science* (Baltimore, MD: Johns Hopkins University Press, 2014). For Zabarella, Piccolomini, and Galileo, see Marco Sgarbi, 'What Does a Renaissance Aristotelian Look Like? From Petrarch to Galilei', in *HOPOS: The Journal of the International Society for the History of Philosophy of Science* 7 (2017), 226–45.

References

INTRODUCTION

On the discovery of the site of the Lyceum, see David Blackman, 'Archaeology in Greece, 1996–97', *Archaeological Reports* 43 (1996–7), 8–10. 'Aristotle is terse . . .' is by Jonathan Barnes, in the introduction to *The Complete Works of Aristotle* (Princeton: Princeton University Press, 1984), vol. 1, p. xi. Plato's nickname for Aristotle, 'the mind', is reported in John Philoponus' *De Aeternitate Mundi* 211,25 Rabe; note also *Vita Marciana* 7, reported in Carlo Natali, *Aristotle: His Life and School* (Princeton: Princeton University Press, 2013; orig. Italian 1991), p. 157.

CHAPTER 1: THE CONTEMPLATIVE LIFE

'All humans by nature desire to know' comes from *Metaphysics* 1.1, 980a21. The story of the loss and rediscovery of Aristotle's works is told in Strabo's *Geography* 13.1.54. Heraclitus' 'it is impossible to step into the same river twice' is quoted in Plato's *Cratylus* 402a. On Cratylus wagging his finger, see Aristotle's *Metaphysics* 4.5, 1010a7–15. Aristotle's 'being in so far as it is being' comes from *Metaphysics* 4.1, 1003a21–2; 'being is said in many ways' comes from *Metaphysics* 4.2, 1003a33 (see also *Metaphysics* 6.2, 1026a33–4). The quotation 'if the primary substances did not exist . . .' is from *Categories* 5, 2b5–6. On Babylonian and Egyptian astronomical records, see Simplicius, *In De Caelo* 117, 21–30 Heiberg. The anecdote about Thales is from Plato's *Theaetetus* 174a.

CHAPTER 2: STUDYING NATURE

On the distinction between metaphysics and physics, see *Parts of Animals* 1.1, 640a1–4. The passage 'The crayfish has two teeth . . .' is from *History of Animals* 4.2, 527a1–8. On bees, see *Generation of Animals* 3.10, which is also the source for 'the facts have not been sufficiently ascertained . . .' (760b30–32). The quotation 'in all natural things there is something marvellous' is from *Parts of Animals* 1.5, 645a16–17. 'A corpse has the same shape and structure as a living body . . .' is from *Parts of Animals* 1.1, 640b33–5. Plato's function argument is in *Republic* 352d–353e. For an outline of Democritean atomism, see *Metaphysics* 1.4, 985b4–20. The passage 'If we were describing a bed . . .' is from *Parts of Animals* 1.1, 640b23–9. 'It may be that the form of any living creature is soul . . .' is from *Parts of Animals* 1.1, 641a17–19. For 'the soul is as it were the first principle of animal life', see *De Anima* 1.1, 402a6–7. 'The soul is the first actuality . . .' is from *De Anima* 2.1, 412a27–8, and 'what it is to be an axe . . .' is from *De Anima* 2.1, 412b12–13. On the final cause as 'that for the sake of which', see *Physics* 2.3, 194b32–3. 'The builder sets before himself . . .' is from *Parts of Animals* 1.1, 639b16–18, and the passage following it is from 639b19–21. On Empedocles and evolution, see *Parts of Animals* 1.1, 640a19–21, and *Physics* 2.4, 196a23–4; for Anaximander, see Plutarch, *Table Talk* 730d–f (translated in Jonathan Barnes, *Early Greek Philosophy*, Harmondsworth: Penguin, 1987, pp. 73–4). Armand Marie Leroi's discussion of the four causes is in *The Lagoon: How Aristotle Invented Science* (London: Bloomsbury, 2014), p. 92. Aristotle's 'the body as a whole must exist . . .' is from *Parts of Animals* 1.5, 645b15–20. 'The function of human beings . . .' is from *Nicomachean Ethics* 1.7, 1098a7.

CHAPTER 3: A RATIONAL ANIMAL

On *logos* and language, see *Politics* 1.2, 1253a7–18. The opening chapter of the *Categories* is 1a1–15. The ten categories are listed at *Categories* 4, 1b25–8. The fourfold distinction between written words, spoken words, thoughts, and things is at *On Interpretation* 1, 16a4–9. 'Someone may predict an event . . .' is from *On Interpretation* 9, 18b33–6, and the passage following it is from 19a1–3. 'What is must be *when* it is . . .' is from *On Interpretation* 9, 19a23–7. The valid argument forms are detailed in *Prior Analytics* 1.4–6. Aristotle comments on dialectical reasoning in *Topics* 1.1, especially 100a18–21. On deductive proofs and ethics, see *Nicomachean Ethics* 1.3, 1094b11–27.

CHAPTER 4: SOCIAL ANIMALS

On Aristotle's love of reading, see *Vita Marciana* 6, quoted in Carlo Natali, *Aristotle: His Life and School* (Princeton: Princeton University Press, 2013; orig. Italian 1991), p. 157. On humans as social animals, see *Politics* 1.2, 1253a2–3. The quotation from Thomas Hobbes comes from *Leviathan*, chapter 13 (London: Andrew Crooke, 1651, p. 62). The passage 'hold it to be indefensible . . .' is from *Politics* 1.6, 1255a9–11; the following one is at 1255b14–15. On the superior perception of women, see *De Anima* 2.9, 421a23–6. For the community being 'prior to the individual', see *Politics* 1.2, 1253a25–6. 'The result is a State not of free men . . .' is from *Politics* 4.11, 1295b21–3, and the passage following it is from 1295b25–6. 'A young man is not a proper hearer . . .' is from *Nicomachean Ethics* 1.3, 1095a2–8.

CHAPTER 5: THE BENEFITS OF LITERATURE

On Aristotle's interests in drama and poetry, see *Poetics* 1, 1447a8–10. On imitation, see *Poetics* 3, 1448a28–9. On developments added by Aeschylus and Sophocles, see *Poetics* 4, 1449a15–19. For plot lines being 'contrary to expectation . . .', see *Poetics* 9, 1452a3–4; the example of 'the statue of Mitys . . .' is at 1452a7–9. For the emotional release of *catharsis*, see *Poetics* 6, 1449b24–8, combined with *Politics* 8.7. The guide to screenwriting mentioned is Robert McKee, *Story: Substance, Structure, Style and the Principles of Screenwriting* (London: Methuen, 1998), p. 5. Aristotle says he will discuss comedy at *Poetics* 6, 1449b21–2, and he mentions his discussion in his *Rhetoric* at 1.11, 1371b33–1372a2, and 3.18, 1419b2–7. The two-book *Poetics* is listed in Diogenes Laertius, *Lives of the Eminent Philosophers* 5.24. Aristotle's few comments on comedy in the *Poetics* are at 1, 1447a13–16, and 13, 1453a38–9. He discusses the virtue of wit in *Nicomachean Ethics* 4.8. On comedy not causing pain, see *Poetics* 5, 1449a34–7. For the comparison of poetry with history, see *Poetics* 9, 1451b4–6.

CHAPTER 6: A GOOD LIFE

Aristotle's definition 'activity of the soul in accordance with reason' is from *Nicomachean Ethics* 1.7, 1098a7. The intellectual virtues are listed at *Nicomachean Ethics* 6.3, 1139b16–17. The table of virtues and vices is at

Eudemian Ethics 2.3, 1220b38–1221a12. The passage 'It is a difficult business to be good . . .' is from *Nicomachean Ethics* 2.9, 1109a24–30. 'It is not easy to define by a rule . . .' is from *Nicomachean Ethics* 2.9, 1109b20–21. The Delphic maxim 'nothing in excess' is recorded in Plato's *Charmides* 165a. Plato refers to a middle path at *Republic* 619a. For the Buddha's turn to the middle way, see the *Life of the Buddha* by Ashvaghosha, translated in Edward Conze, *Buddhist Scriptures* (Harmondsworth: Penguin, 1959), especially pp. 46–7. Confucius' 'the mean is supreme' is from *Analects* 6.29. On happiness as an activity (and so incompatible with being asleep), see *Nicomachean Ethics* 10.6. On contemplation being the life of a god, see *Nicomachean Ethics* 10.7.

CHAPTER 7: A LIFE OF INQUIRY

Plato's comment on Xenocrates and Aristotle is reported in Diogenes Laertius, *Lives of the Eminent Philosophers* 4.6. Theophrastus' use of maps is also reported in Diogenes Laertius, at 5.51, as is Aristotle's purchase of the books of Speusippus, at 4.5. On the necessity of leisure, see *Nicomachean Ethics* 10.7. On Athens sinning against philosophy a second time, see *Vita Marciana* 41, cited in Carlo Natali's *Aristotle: His Life and School* (Princeton: Princeton University Press, 2013; orig. Italian, 1991), p. 63. On Aristotle teaching in Chalcis, see Diogenes Laertius 10.1. On Demetrius of Phalerum's help securing the property of the Lyceum, see Diogenes Laertius 5.39. Francis Bacon comments 'knowledge derived from Aristotle . . .' in *The Advancement of Learning* 1.4.12 (ed. William Aldis Wright, Oxford: Clarendon Press, 1869, p. 37). The quotations from Piccolomini and Galileo come from Marco Sgarbi, 'What Does a Renaissance Aristotelian Look Like? From Petrarch to Galilei', in *HOPOS: The Journal of the International Society for the History of Philosophy of Science* 7 (2017), pp. 237 and 240. On Aristotle's 'excessive tentativeness . . .', see Richard Robinson, *Aristotle's Politics: Books III and IV* (Oxford: Clarendon Press, 1962), p. viii. Aristotle comments on being a greater friend of truth than of Plato in *Nicomachean Ethics* 1.6, 1096a11–17.

Acknowledgements

I thank my editor at Penguin, Casiana Ionita, for supporting this project, Edward Kirke for his astute comments on the manuscript, Kit Shepherd for his meticulous copyediting, along with everyone else at Penguin who has contributed to making this book a reality. As a curious teenager, keen to learn more, practically all the books I read that started me off on the path that I am still on today were affordable and widely available Penguin paperbacks. Few organizations have done more to open the world of learning to a wide audience and so I am delighted to be a Penguin author, now for the third time.

As always, I thank my wife Dawn, who both read the final manuscript, as she does with almost everything I write, catching numerous errors that no one else noticed, and patiently listened to me talk about Aristotle for many months beforehand.

It also gives me great pleasure to thank Sir Richard Sorabji, one of the pre-eminent Aristotelians of his generation, who, with his characteristic generosity, found time to read my manuscript despite many other competing demands. His expert eye has given this book a degree of precision it would not otherwise have had. It has been a great privilege to have worked with Richard on his project devoted to the ancient commentators on Aristotle on and off for a good part of the last twenty years. I have learned so much from his example over these years and benefited in numerous ways from his support and guidance, which, at some junctures, have been crucial. With sincere thanks, I dedicate this book to Richard.

Index

PELICAN BOOKS

PELICAN BOOKS

PELICAN BOOKS

PELICAN BOOKS

Architecture:
From Prehistory to Climate Emergency
Barnabas Calder

Covid by Numbers:
Making Sense of the Pandemic with Data
David Spiegelhalter and Anthony Masters

Around the World in 80 Books
David Damrosch

How Religion Evolved:
And Why It Endures
Robin Dunbar

The Blue Commons:
Rescuing the Economy of the Sea
Guy Standing

The Holocaust:
An Unfinished History
Dan Stone

Aristotle:
Understanding the World's Greatest Philosopher
John Sellars

The Power of Language:
Multilingualism, Self and Society
Viorica Marian

Traditionalism:
The Radical Project for Restoring Sacred Order
Mark Sedgwick

'A great way into one of the greatest philosophers of all time' NIGEL WARBURTON

Why has Aristotle had such an astounding influence on the world?

What are his key ideas?

What can he still teach us today?

John Sellars is Reader in Philosophy at Royal Holloway, University of London, a Visiting Research Fellow at King's College London and a Member of Common Room at Wolfson College, Oxford. His books include *Lessons in Stoicism* and *The Fourfold Remedy*, which have been translated into over a dozen languages.

'A delightful little book' JIM AL-KHALILI

'A brilliantly clear introduction to the whole range of his thought' ROBERT EAGLESTONE

ISBN 978-0-241-61564-5

U.K. £9.99
CAN. $21.99
A PELICAN BOOK
Cover by Matthew Young

9 780241 615645

62199

FSC

The
Freedom
to Be
Free

Hannah
Arendt

'People can only be free
in relation to one another'

Penguin Books   Great Ideas